Civil War Politics: The Divided Nation And Its Leaders

Mokhtari Behzad

Published by Mokhtari Behzad, 2024.

CIVIL WAR POLITICS: THE DIVIDED NATION AND ITS LEADERS

First edition. May 14, 2024.

ISBN: 979-8224235544

Written by Mokhtari Behzad.

Table of Contents

Chapter 1: Introduction

OVERVIEW OF THE CIVIL War

One of the main causes of the Civil War was the issue of slavery. Slavery was deeply rooted in the Southern states, where it was an integral part of the agricultural economy. The Northern states, on the other hand, had largely abolished slavery, favoring industrialization and a free labor system. As the United States expanded westward, the question of whether new territories would allow slavery or not became increasingly contentious. This issue reached a boiling point with the 1860 election of Abraham Lincoln, a Republican who called for limiting the spread of slavery. This election, coupled with Southern fears of losing their way of life, ultimately led to the secession of several states and the formation of the Confederacy.

The first shots of the Civil War were fired at Fort Sumter in South Carolina on April 12, 1861. This event marked the beginning of a long and bloody conflict that would rage for four years. The war was characterized by major battles fought on both sides, including the Battle of Gettysburg, Antietam, and Bull Run. These battles brought immense loss of life and devastation, with soldiers fighting for their cause in treacherous conditions. The Union army, led by General Ulysses S. Grant, eventually gained the upper hand over the Confederates, but not without significant sacrifice and struggle.

Aside from the major battles, the Civil War also saw the implementation of new tactics and technologies. Both sides utilized the latest weaponry, including rifled muskets, artillery, and ironclad warships. The naval battle between the Union ironclad, the USS Monitor, and the Confederate ironclad, the CSS Virginia, was a landmark moment in naval warfare. The use of trenches and entrenchments, as well as the construction of fortifications, became prevalent as the war dragged on and both sides sought strategic advantages.

The aftermath of the Civil War brought significant changes to American society. Slavery was officially abolished with the passage of the Thirteenth

Amendment in 1865, marking a turning point in the fight for civil rights. The period of Reconstruction that followed aimed to rebuild the South and integrate freed slaves into society. However, Reconstruction was not without its challenges, including resistance from former Confederates and the rise of white supremacist groups such as the Ku Klux Klan. The scars of the war, both physical and emotional, lingered for generations, creating a lasting impact on American identity and the understanding of civil rights. It was a conflict born out of the divisions between the Northern and Southern states, with slavery at the core of the dispute. The war brought immense loss of life and devastation, but it also marked the beginning of a new era in the fight for civil rights. The legacy of the Civil War continues to shape America today, highlighting the importance of unity, empathy, and a commitment to equality. By understanding the causes, events, and aftermath of the Civil War, we can gain a deeper appreciation for the challenges overcome by this nation and the ongoing struggle towards a more perfect union.

Causes of the Civil War

It resulted in unprecedented casualties, political and economic upheaval, and ultimately the preservation of the Union. Understanding the causes of this complex conflict is crucial for evaluating its impact and developing a comprehensive perspective. In this analysis, we will explore the multifaceted factors that contributed to the outbreak of the Civil War. By examining political, economic, and social elements, we aim to shed light on the deep-rooted causes that led to this monumental conflict.

Political Causes:

Political discord played a prominent role in the underlying tensions preceding the Civil War. The foremost issue was the divide between the industrialized Northern states and the agrarian Southern states. Conflicts arose over various matters, including the rights of states, the expansion of slavery into western territories, and the role of the federal government. The Missouri Compromise of 1820 temporarily eased tensions by admitting Missouri as a slave state while imposing a line, prohibiting slavery north of the 36°30′ parallel. However, subsequent legislative attempts to maintain the balance between free and slave states, including the Kansas-Nebraska Act and the Dred Scott decision, only exacerbated sectional polarization.

CIVIL WAR POLITICS: THE DIVIDED NATION AND ITS LEADERS

Economic Causes:

Economic disparities between the North and the South also played a critical role in precipitating the Civil War. The North experienced rapid industrialization, resulting in a growing middle class and increased urbanization. Meanwhile, the South relied heavily on its cash crop-driven, slave-based plantation economy. As the North embraced technological advancements and pursued protective tariffs to foster domestic industries, the South found its agricultural production increasingly dependent on slavery. This divergent economic trajectory further deepened the rift between the two regions, creating conflicting interests and exacerbating divisions.

Social Causes:

Slavery, the most contentious issue of the era, represented the most pronounced social cause underlying the Civil War. Slavery had been an integral part of the Southern economy and society since the colonial era. Abolitionist movements, gaining momentum within the Northern states, fueled tensions by challenging the moral, ethical, and economic justifications for human bondage. Social reform movements, such as the Underground Railroad and the publication of influential anti-slavery works like Uncle Tom's Cabin, aroused passions on both sides. Slavery's impact on the social fabric of an increasingly uncertain nation served as a catalyst for heightened sectionalism in the years leading up to the Civil War.

Sectionalism:

We cannot fully understand the causes of the Civil War without considering the deep-rooted sectionalism that divided the nation. Sectional differences emerged due to geographic, economic, and cultural disparities between the North and the South. These differences manifested in contrasting societal structures, political interests, and moral values. The North's embrace of industrialization, free labor, and reform movements clashed with the South's staunch defense of agricultural dependency, slaveholding, and traditional social hierarchies. Expanding westward, the question of whether new territories would permit slavery intensified the sectional divide and ignited passionate debates.

Breakdown of Compromise:

The breakdown of longstanding compromise measures further exacerbated tensions and escalated the likelihood of armed conflict. Decades of political maneuvering and temporary solutions, such as the Missouri Compromise and the Compromise of 1850, gradually eroded trust and raised fundamental questions about the nation's ability to reconcile its moral and economic differences. The election of President Abraham Lincoln, a staunch opponent of the expansion of slavery, became a tipping point for secession. South Carolina led the way by nullifying federal authority and was soon followed by ten other Southern states, leading to the establishment of the Confederate States of America. The division between the Union and the Confederacy marked the start of the Civil War.

EXAMINING THE CAUSES of the American Civil War reveals a complex tapestry of political, economic, social, and sectional factors. Deep-rooted disagreements over slavery, the balance of power between states and the federal government, and disparities in industrialization and agriculture all contributed to the nation's descent into armed conflict. Understanding the causes of this devastating war provides valuable insights into the challenges faced by a young nation striving to define its identity and reconcile its differences. By learning from history, we can better navigate the complexities of our present and shape a more inclusive and united future.

Introduction to key leaders

In any field or industry, key leaders play a crucial role in shaping the direction and success of a particular organization or movement. These leaders possess a unique set of skills, expertise, and personal qualities that inspire and motivate others to achieve their goals. This book aims to provide an introduction to some of history's most prominent key leaders, exploring their leadership styles, achievements, and contributions. Whether you are a student, aspiring leader, or someone with a general interest in leadership, this book will offer insights into the lives of these influential figures and help you gain a deeper understanding of their impact on their respective fields.

Leadership is a complex and multi-faceted concept that has captivated scholars and practitioners for centuries. It is commonly defined as the ability to influence, guide, and direct individuals or groups towards a common goal. Key leaders possess this ability in abundance, and their impact can be seen in various aspects of society, such as politics, business, and social movements.

One of the key leaders we will explore in this book is Mahatma Gandhi. Gandhi, born in 1869 in British India, is widely regarded as one of the greatest leaders in history. He championed nonviolent civil disobedience as a means to achieve social and political change, leading India to gain independence from British rule. Gandhi's leadership style was characterized by his emphasis on moral and ethical principles, simplicity, and self-discipline. His unwavering commitment to nonviolence and his ability to mobilize masses through peaceful protests and acts of civil disobedience paved the way for India's liberation and influenced leaders and movements worldwide.

Another key leader we will examine is Nelson Mandela. Mandela, born in South Africa in 1918, was a prominent anti-apartheid activist who became the country's first black president in 1994. Mandela's leadership was marked by his unwavering determination, resilience, and commitment to justice and equality. Despite being imprisoned for 27 years, Mandela emerged as a symbol of reconciliation and unity, advocating for nonviolence and promoting racial harmony in a divided society. His visionary leadership and ability to bring people together were instrumental in dismantling the apartheid regime and laying the foundation for a democratic South Africa.

Moving beyond political leaders, we will also delve into the realm of business leadership and explore figures such as Steve Jobs. Jobs, the co-founder of Apple Inc., revolutionized the technology industry with his visionary ideas and relentless pursuit of excellence. Known for his charismatic and demanding leadership style, Jobs pushed the boundaries of innovation and created products that transformed the way we interact with technology. His ability to inspire and motivate his team, along with his relentless pursuit of perfection, propelled Apple to become one of the most valuable companies in the world. Jobs' leadership style serves as a testament to the importance of embracing creativity, thinking differently, and challenging the status quo.

Additionally, we will discuss the leadership of Malala Yousafzai, a Pakistani activist and Nobel laureate. Yousafzai, born in 1997, became a global symbol of education and women's rights after surviving an assassination attempt by the Taliban for advocating for girls' education in her native Swat Valley. Yousafzai's leadership is characterized by her resilience, courage, and passion for empowering youth. Despite facing adversity, she continues to fight for universal access to education, becoming a voice for millions of children and inspiring young people worldwide to stand up for what they believe in.

These are just a few examples of the key leaders we will explore in this book. By analyzing their leadership styles, accomplishments, and legacies, we hope to shed light on the qualities and principles that define effective leadership. Ultimately, our goal is to inspire and educate readers about the power of leadership and its potential to shape the course of history. Whether you are a student seeking to learn from the great leaders of the past or an aspiring leader looking for guidance, this book will provide valuable insights into the lives and leadership journeys of these exceptional individuals.

Chapter 2: The Antebellum Era

POLITICAL CLIMATE LEADING up to the Civil War

In the years following the American Revolution, the North and the South had developed separate economies, largely driven by their different approaches to agriculture. The North, with its fertile soil and abundant natural resources, embraced industrialization and became an economic powerhouse. On the other hand, the South relied heavily on the labor-intensive cultivation of cotton and other cash crops, relying heavily on slave labor. This fundamental difference in economic systems would play a significant role in shaping the political landscape leading up to the Civil War.

As the United States expanded westward, the question of whether new territories would be admitted as free or slave states became a contentious issue. The Missouri Compromise of 1820 had temporarily resolved this issue by drawing a line across the continent, allowing slavery to expand below the line but prohibiting it above. However, as more territories were acquired through the Mexican-American War and the Louisiana Purchase, the extension of slavery into these new lands became a subject of bitter debate in Congress.

The passage of the Compromise of 1850, which admitted California as a free state but also strengthened the Fugitive Slave Law, further heightened tensions between the North and the South. The Fugitive Slave Law required Northern states to return escaped slaves to their owners, causing outrage among abolitionists and intensifying calls for an end to slavery. This controversial law served as a catalyst for the burgeoning abolitionist movement in the North, increasing animosity between the two regions.

Another contentious issue during this time was the concept of states' rights. Southern states argued that each state had the right to determine the legality of slavery within its own borders, while the federal government argued for a more centralized approach. This clash between the principles of federalism and states' rights became a central point of contention leading up to the Civil War.

The political climate leading up to the Civil War was further exacerbated by the emergence of new political parties and the rise of charismatic leaders. The Whig Party, which had been a major political force in the early 19th century, began to fracture as North-South divisions deepened. The party's collapse gave rise to the Republican Party, which largely represented the interests of the industrial North and embraced anti-slavery sentiments. The Democratic Party, on the other hand, was divided along regional lines, with Northern Democrats generally opposed to the expansion of slavery and Southern Democrats advocating for its preservation.

Perhaps the most significant event leading up to the Civil War was the election of Abraham Lincoln as President in 1860. His election on a platform that opposed the spread of slavery to new territories was met with outrage in the South. Southern states, fearing that their way of life was under threat, began to secede from the Union, forming the Confederate States of America. The stage was set for a bloody conflict that would determine the future of the nation. The expansion of slavery, the preservation of states' rights, and the rise of new political parties all contributed to the growing divide. Ultimately, the election of Abraham Lincoln as President and the subsequent secession of Southern states set in motion a chain of events that would lead to the bloodiest conflict in American history. Understanding this complex political landscape is crucial to unraveling the causes and consequences of the Civil War.

Debate over slavery

To begin understanding the debate over slavery, it is important to delve into its origins. Slavery traces its roots back to ancient civilizations, where it was a common practice adopted by various societies. However, as human societies progressed and developed more sophisticated legal and ethical frameworks, opinions on slavery started to diverge. Some argued that it was an essential institution for economic prosperity, while others believed it was a gross violation of human dignity.

During the 18th and 19th centuries, the debate over slavery took center stage, particularly in Western societies. The emergence of the Enlightenment and the principles of individual freedom and natural rights led to the questioning of the moral legitimacy of slavery. Enlightenment thinkers, such as John Locke and Jean-Jacques Rousseau, argued that every individual had inherent rights including life, liberty, and property, irrespective of their race or social status. These ideas laid the groundwork for arguments against slavery, positing that it was a direct violation of these fundamental human rights.

On the other hand, proponents of slavery put forth various arguments to defend its practice. Economic considerations played a significant role in these justifications. Slavery was seen as an essential aspect of the plantation system, which allowed for the production of valuable goods such as sugar, tobacco, and cotton. Advocates of slavery argued that this system boosted economic development, arguing that such progress outweighed any moral concerns. Additionally, racist ideologies were also invoked to perpetuate the institution of slavery. People of African descent were often deemed inferior and therefore, it was argued, justified to be enslaved.

Moving forward in history, the debate over slavery reached a tipping point in the 19th century, particularly in the United States. The expansion of the nation westward reignited the discussion on whether new territories should permit slavery or not. This dispute led to heightened tensions between Northern states, where abolitionist sentiment was gaining momentum, and the Southern states, which heavily relied on slave labor for their agrarian-based economy.

The debate over slavery became increasingly polarized, culminating in the American Civil War. Pro-abolition forces fought to end the institution of slavery, viewing it as a morally reprehensible practice that contradicted the principles upon which the United States was founded. Ultimately, after a long and bloody conflict, slavery was abolished in the United States with the ratification of the Thirteenth Amendment in 1865. This important historical milestone marked the beginning of a new one in the struggle for racial equality.

While the debate over slavery officially ended in the United States with its abolition, the ramifications and legacy of slavery continue to reverberate through society and shape contemporary discussions on race, inequality, and justice. The wounds inflicted by centuries of enslaved labor, racial discrimination, and systemic oppression are deep and enduring. This book aims to provide a comprehensive understanding of the historical and intellectual underpinnings of the debate over slavery, serving as a starting point for readers to engage with these complex issues and contribute to ongoing conversations surrounding equality and social justice. The clash between those who advocated for its abolition on moral and ethical grounds and those who defended its economic and racist justifications shaped the trajectory of nations and continues to impact society today. Understanding the multifaceted arguments and perspectives surrounding this debate is essential in order to grapple with the historical, social, and moral implications of slavery, and to work towards a more inclusive and just future. Through examining the origins, Enlightenment influences, economic justifications, and ultimate abolition, this book aims to present a comprehensive and thought-provoking exploration of this important historical topic.

Key events leading to the outbreak of war

Wars rarely arise from isolated incidents but are often the result of a complex web of interactions, tensions, and conflicts that gradually build up over time. This exploration aims to shed light on the significant historical events leading up to the outbreak of war, highlighting their interconnectedness and the subsequent impact on global politics, economies, and societies. By unraveling these complex dynamics, we can gain valuable insights into the factors that culminate in violent conflicts. This exploration will primarily focus on the causes behind major historical wars and analyze their impacts from a professional and academic standpoint, while maintaining an approachable and friendly tone throughout the discourse.

1. The Treaty of Versailles and the Fallout from World War I:

The conclusion of World War I witnessed the signing of the Treaty of Versailles in 1919, which sought to impose harsh reparations and territorial adjustments upon Germany. The punitive nature of the treaty deeply humiliated the German populace and inflicted significant economic burdens. Such deficiencies bred resentment and sowed the seeds for the rise of radical ideologieslike Nazism in Germany, ultimately paving the way for the outbreak of World War II.

2. Failure of Diplomatic Means:

Another key factor leading to the outbreak of war is the failure of diplomatic channels in resolving tensions. Diplomatic efforts, such as treaties, negotiations, and peace conferences, often unravel due to the rigid standpoints of nations involved or the inability to compromise. The failure of such diplomatic means was particularly evident in the lead-up to World War II, where the appeasement policy towards Nazi Germany failed to rein in Hitler's expansionist ambitions, ultimately escalating tensions to the point of war.

3. The Rise of Nationalism and Imperialism:

Throughout history, the rise of nationalism and imperialism has often acted as a catalyst for conflicts. The quest for power, resources, and territorial control has frequently fueled rivalries between nations and has ultimately led to war. For instance, the events leading up to World War I were significantly influenced by the competing imperialist ambitions of European powers, as well as growing nationalist movements seeking self-determination.

4. Economic Rivalries and Trade Wars:

Economic rivalries and trade wars can also play a significant role in precipitating conflicts. As nations vie for limited resources and economic dominance, tensions can escalate into full-blown warfare. The interwar period leading to World War II witnessed economic rivalries stemming from protectionist policies, currency wars, and the Great Depression. These economic struggles contributed to national frustration, exacerbating the likelihood of war.

5. Ethnic, Religious, and Cultural Conflicts:

Ethnic, religious, and cultural conflicts are often deeply rooted in historical animosities and can serve as a potent catalyst for war. Conflicts arising from differing ethnic or religious identities, discriminatory practices, or territorial disputes can quickly escalate into large-scale violence. Examples include the Balkan Wars of the early 20th century, which were fueled by ethnic tensions resulting from the dissolution of the Ottoman Empire.

6. Miscalculations and the Escalation Spiral:

The outbreak of war can sometimes stem from a series of miscalculations, misinterpretations, and miscommunications among nations. Such misunderstandings can lead to rapid escalation as each side misjudges the intentions and capabilities of their adversaries. This largely contributed to the outbreak of World War I, as nations were drawn into a catastrophic conflict due to a series of diplomatic failures, miscalculations, and the rapid mobilization of military forces.

UNDERSTANDING THE KEY events leading to the outbreak of war requires a comprehensive analysis of historical, political, economic, and social factors. The Treaty of Versailles, diplomatic failures, the rise of nationalism, economic rivalries, ethnoreligious conflicts, and miscalculations all play significant roles in shaping the path towards war. By critically examining these events and their interconnections, we can gain valuable insights into the complex dynamics and multifaceted causes that contribute to the eruption of violent conflicts. Ultimately, such an understanding is paramount in our pursuit of peaceful coexistence and conflict prevention in the future.

Chapter 3: Abraham Lincoln: The Great Emancipator

LINCOLN'S RISE TO POWER

From his humble beginnings to becoming one of the most revered presidents in American history, Lincoln's ascent to power is a testament to his vision, determination, and unwavering leadership. This exploration will delve into the key milestones, strategies, and qualities that propelled Lincoln from a relatively unknown Illinois lawyer to the influential and transformative leader he became during his presidency.

Background and Early Life

To understand Lincoln's rise to power, it is essential to examine his background and early life. Born in a modest log cabin in Kentucky in 1809, Lincoln faced numerous challenges and hardships. The loss of his mother at a young age and his father's limited education meant that Lincoln had to seek knowledge and self-improvement independently. Despite these circumstances, Lincoln developed a deep passion for learning, fostered by his voracious reading habits and a deep understanding of the power of education.

Legal and Political Career

Lincoln's early political aspirations and legal career played vital roles in his path to power. Graduating from law school and establishing a successful practice in Illinois, Lincoln gained valuable experience and honed his public speaking skills. His political career began as a Whig politician, serving in the Illinois General Assembly and later the U.S. House of Representatives. These experiences allowed Lincoln to cultivate relationships, learn the intricacies of politics, and sharpen his understanding of the issues facing the nation.

The Road to the Presidency

Lincoln's rise to the presidency was marked by his firm stance against slavery, a defining issue of the time. The Lincoln-Douglas debates of 1858, in which Lincoln challenged Senator Stephen A. Douglas, catapulted him to national prominence. Though he lost the Senate race, Lincoln's compelling arguments against slavery resonated throughout the country, positioning him as a leading voice within the Republican Party. Ultimately, his successful campaign for the presidency in 1860 solidified his climb to power and set the stage for the challenges he would soon face.

Leadership During the Civil War

Lincoln's presidency coincided with one of the most tumultuous periods in American history—the Civil War. During this critical time, Lincoln's leadership would be tested as he navigated the complexities of war, political divides, and the preservation of the Union. Lincoln's ability to inspire, unite, and make challenging decisions earned him the respect and loyalty of both his advisors and the American people. By constantly seeking the counsel of experts and providing unwavering support to his generals, Lincoln displayed remarkable leadership traits that influenced the outcome of the war.

Emancipation Proclamation and the Legacy of Freedom

One of the defining moments in Lincoln's rise to power was the Emancipation Proclamation, issued in 1862. This landmark document declared the freedom of slaves in Confederate territory and fundamentally transformed the purpose of the Civil War. While its immediate impact was limited, the Emancipation Proclamation set the stage for the Thirteenth Amendment and the eventual abolishment of slavery. Lincoln's unwavering commitment to justice and equality contributed to his everlasting legacy as a champion of freedom.

ABRAHAM LINCOLN'S RISE to power is a testament to his unwavering determination, intellectual rigor, and exceptional leadership during a pivotal period in American history. From his modest beginnings to his courageous stance against slavery, Lincoln's transformative journey exemplifies the power of individual beliefs and actions. By examining Lincoln's background, political career, and leadership during the Civil War, we gain invaluable insights that remain relevant and inspiring today. Lincoln's rise to power serves as a reminder that true leaders are capable of shaping history and making lasting positive change in the face of adversity.

Lincoln's leadership during the war

One of the defining qualities of Lincoln's leadership was his ability to navigate the complex landscape of politics during a time of intense turmoil. As the country found itself embroiled in a bloody civil war, Lincoln had to balance his role as a commander-in-chief with being the leader of a politically divided nation. His adeptness at coalition-building and his willingness to listen to conflicting opinions allowed him to bring together individuals from different backgrounds and parties in pursuit of a common goal. Lincoln recognized that success in war required a united front, and through skillful negotiations and strategic appointments, he was able to assemble a team that could collectively confront the challenges ahead.

Another crucial aspect of Lincoln's leadership was his unwavering commitment to the principle of equality. Despite being a product of his time, Lincoln held a deep conviction that all individuals, regardless of their race or background, deserved equal rights and opportunities. This guiding ethos shaped his policies and decisions throughout the war. From his famous Emancipation Proclamation to the establishment of the Thirteenth Amendment, Lincoln's leadership laid the foundation for the eventual abolition of slavery and the advancement of civil rights in the United States. His steadfast belief in the value of every human being resonates even today and serves as a timeless reminder of the power of inclusive leadership.

Furthermore, Lincoln's leadership during the war can be characterized by his integrity and fortitude in the face of adversity. As the war raged on, Lincoln faced numerous setbacks and challenges that tested his resolve. However, he remained resolute in his commitment to preserving the Union and upholding the principles upon which the country was founded. Through his speeches and letters, Lincoln inspired the nation to persevere and endure the hardships brought about by the war. His ability to rally the American people behind a common cause, even amidst the darkest of times, demonstrated his unmatched leadership qualities.

In addition to his exceptional leadership abilities, Lincoln was known for his strategic thinking and diplomatic finesse. He understood the necessity of devising innovative approaches to win the war while minimizing casualties. The appointment of capable military commanders such as Ulysses S. Grant and the implementation of the Anaconda Plan showcased Lincoln's ability to adapt military strategies to changing circumstances. His willingness to listen to military advice and embrace unconventional tactics allowed the Union forces to gain the upper hand, ultimately contributing to their victory.

Moreover, Lincoln's leadership during the war was characterized by his emphasis on national unity and reconciliation. Even as the conflict drew to a close, he recognized the need to heal the wounds inflicted by the war and rebuild a war-torn nation. Through his lenient approach towards the Confederate states and the issuance of his second inaugural address, Lincoln displayed a remarkable sense of compassion and forgiveness. His vision of a united United States, where both the North and the South could reconcile their differences and move forward, showed his ability to rise above personal grievances and prioritize the greater good of the country. Through his political acumen, commitment to equality, integrity in the face of adversity, strategic thinking, and emphasis on national unity, Lincoln not only guided the Union to victory but also inspired future generations of leaders. His incredible story serves as a reminder that leadership is not solely about making the right decisions or achieving short-term goals, but about empowering others, staying true to one's principles, and striving for a better future. Lincoln's leadership during the war continues to inspire and teach valuable lessons, making it a topic of great importance and relevance.

Chapter 4: Jefferson Davis: President of the Confederacy

DAVIS'S POLITICAL CAREER

Born into a middle-class family in a small town, Davis's interest in politics was sparked at a young age. His first foray into public service came during his college years, where he became actively involved in student government. This early involvement laid the foundation for his future political ambitions and provided him with valuable experience in grassroots organization and leadership.

After completing his studies, Davis decided to enter local politics. Starting as a city council member, he quickly gained a reputation for being a diligent and dedicated public servant. His ability to address constituent concerns and tackle local issues catapulted him into higher positions within the municipal government. Davis's significant accomplishments in this role included spearheading economic development initiatives, improving public infrastructure, and promoting social welfare programs.

Building on his success at the local level, Davis soon set his eyes on a higher office. His charisma, intellect, and strong work ethic propelled him through a competitive campaign for a seat in the state legislature. Elected by a narrow margin, Davis earned the trust of his constituents through tireless advocacy and his unwavering commitment to their needs. During his time in the state legislature, Davis sponsored and supported legislation that aimed to improve education, strengthen environmental protections, and champion social justice causes. His dedication to these issues helped him gain support from both sides of the political spectrum and solidify his reputation as a pragmatic and effective legislator.

Davis's skillful leadership and his tireless dedication to public service did not go unnoticed on the national stage. Recognizing his potential, national party leaders encouraged Davis to pursue a seat in Congress. Although hesitant at first, Davis eventually embraced the challenge and ran a spirited campaign that won him a seat in the House of Representatives. As a member of Congress, Davis proved to be a formidable lawmaker, tirelessly advocating for the interests of his district and constituents. His legislative successes included passing comprehensive healthcare reform, advocating for stronger gun control measures, and championing bipartisan initiatives aimed at addressing economic inequality.

Despite his numerous accomplishments, Davis faced his fair share of challenges throughout his political career. He weathered political scandals, contentious debates, and personal attacks with grace and resilience. Davis's ability to navigate difficult circumstances and maintain his integrity and focus on his constituents' needs earned him respect from both colleagues and the general public.

Throughout his political career, Davis's commitment to public service remained steadfast. He tirelessly fought for equal opportunities, social justice, and economic prosperity for all. His ability to connect with people from all walks of life and understand their concerns made him a beloved figure among voters. From his early days in local government to his time in Congress, Davis consistently demonstrated his commitment to enacting positive change. Through his legislative achievements, personal integrity, and unwavering dedication to his constituents, Davis's impact on the political landscape will be remembered for generations to come.

Formation of the Confederacy

The roots of the Confederacy can be traced back to the issue of slavery, which had long been a contentious topic in the United States. The Southern states heavily relied on slave labor for their agrarian-based economies, while the Northern states increasingly embraced industrialization and a more diversified economy. As the North grew stronger economically and politically, tensions between the regions escalated, ultimately leading to a profound divide between the pro-slavery South and the anti-slavery North.

By the late 1850s, the issue of slavery had become a central point of conflict, as compromises and legal measures attempting to address the matter only served to deepen the divide between the Northern and Southern states. The election of Republican candidate Abraham Lincoln as the president in 1860 further intensified the situation. Many Southerners saw Lincoln's election as a threat to their way of life and the institution of slavery.

South Carolina became the first state to secede from the Union on December 20, 1860. Following South Carolina's lead, six more Southern states seceded by February 1861: Mississippi, Florida, Alabama, Georgia, Louisiana, and Texas. These seceding states convened in Montgomery, Alabama, in February 1861 to form the Confederate States of America. Delegates from each state drafted a constitution and elected Jefferson Davis as the president of the Confederacy.

The formation of the Confederacy was driven by several key motivations. First and foremost was the preservation of slavery, as it formed the backbone of the Southern economy and the social fabric of the region. Many Southern leaders saw secession as the only means to protect their "peculiar institution" and maintain the power dynamics that had been in place for generations.

Additionally, a desire for state sovereignty played a significant role in the formation of the Confederacy. Southern states believed in the principle of states' rights, which held that the federal government should have limited power, with states having the authority to govern themselves independently. They feared that the growing influence of the federal government, particularly under President Lincoln, would encroach upon their autonomy.

Economic factors also contributed to the formation of the Confederacy. The South relied heavily on cotton exports, which accounted for a significant portion of the American economy. Many Southern leaders believed that their economic interests would be best served by breaking away from the industrialized North and forming their own nation with the ability to govern trade and tariffs independently.

The formation of the Confederacy had profound implications for the nation as a whole. It signaled a significant fracture in the United States, with the potential for further divisions and even the dissolution of the Union. The secession of the Southern states ultimately led to the Civil War, one of the bloodiest and most consequential conflicts in American history.

The Confederacy's emergence also had wider international implications, particularly concerning the recognition of the Southern nation by foreign powers. The Confederacy sought support from European countries such as Great Britain and France, hoping that their economic ties to the South would lead to diplomatic recognition. However, the Confederacy's reliance on slave labor made it difficult to garner support from nations that had already abolished slavery and were shifting towards a more progressive stance. Driven by the issues of slavery, state sovereignty, and economic interests, the secession of the Southern states led to the creation of a separate nation and ultimately led to the Civil War. Understanding this critical one in American history allows us to comprehend the complex forces at work and the tensions that ultimately tore the nation apart. By examining the motivations and implications of the Confederacy's formation, we gain a deeper understanding of the struggles and challenges faced by the United States during this critical period.

Challenges faced by the Confederacy

One of the primary challenges faced by the Confederacy was its economic vulnerability. Unlike the industrial North, the South relied heavily on agriculture, primarily cotton, as its economic backbone. This over-reliance on one cash crop left the Confederate economy susceptible to fluctuations in global markets and hindered their ability to supply the necessary resources for the war. The Union blockade also severely impacted the Confederacy's ability to import and export goods, further exacerbating their economic woes. As a result, scarcity of essential goods, inflation, and ultimately economic collapse became prevalent issues that plagued the Confederacy throughout the war.

Another significant challenge faced by the Confederacy was its limited industrial capacity. The South lacked the industrial infrastructure and expertise needed to sustain a protracted war. Unlike the North, which had a well-established industrial base, the Confederacy struggled to produce weapons, ammunition, and other essential war supplies. The scarcity of these resources not only weakened the Confederate army but also undermined their overall war effort. Additionally, the lack of manufacturing facilities hindered the South's ability to repair and maintain their existing weaponry and equipment, further diminishing their military strength.

In addition to economic and industrial challenges, the Confederacy also wrestled with deep-rooted political divisions. Diversity of interests and conflicting ideologies among Confederate leaders created significant obstacles to unity and effective decision-making. Rivalries between individual states' rights and centralized control often hindered effective coordination between the Confederate government and the various states within its jurisdiction. These divisions not only impacted the efficiency and effectiveness of the Confederate government but also created dissension and disunity among the Southern population, further weakening the Confederacy's overall cohesion.

Furthermore, the Confederacy faced significant challenges in terms of manpower and enlistment. Although initially buoyed by a sense of patriotism and a belief in their cause, the enthusiasm for enlisting in the Confederate army dwindled over time. The Confederacy's ability to conscript soldiers was limited, leading to an overreliance on voluntary enlistments. As the war dragged on, enthusiasm waned, and the Confederate army struggled to maintain its numbers. African Americans, who were initially barred from serving in the Confederate army, were only reluctantly accepted as soldiers in the latter stages of the war, further illustrating the Confederacy's challenges in recruiting and retaining manpower.

One of the most glaring challenges faced by the Confederacy was its diplomatic isolation. The Confederate States of America sought recognition and support from foreign nations, primarily European powers, but struggled to gain the international legitimacy they desired. The Union's diplomatic efforts effectively undermined the Confederacy's attempts to obtain foreign aid and recognition. The Lincoln administration skillfully portrayed the conflict as a fight against slavery and secured the support of major powers, such as Britain and France, who had abolished slavery in their own territories. This diplomatic isolation further constrained the Confederacy's ability to acquire essential resources and weakened their overall war effort. The economic vulnerability, limited industrial capacity, and lack of unity hindered the Confederacy's ability to effectively sustain a protracted war. These challenges, coupled with the Union's economic blockade and diplomatic isolation efforts, ultimately contributed to the Confederacy's ultimate defeat. The Confederacy's struggle to overcome these challenges highlights the intricacies of war and the critical role they play in shaping a nation's fate.

Chapter 5: The Battle of Gettysburg

OVERVIEW OF THE BATTLE

The battle was a pivotal moment in the history of warfare, showcasing the strategies and tactics employed by commanders on both sides. It marked a turning point in the larger conflict and had far-reaching consequences for the nations involved. By delving into the details of the battle, we can gain valuable insights into the military capabilities, leadership qualities, and the overall impact it had on the course of history.

To begin, it is essential to establish the context in which the battle took place. This includes discussing the geopolitical situation, the motivations of the parties involved, and the key events leading up to the confrontation. By understanding the background, readers can appreciate the larger significance of the battle and its implications for the wider conflict.

The next aspect to explore is the strategic considerations and objectives of the opposing forces. This involves analyzing the territorial and logistical advantages sought by each side, as well as the overall military strategies employed. By examining the decision-making process of the commanders and the factors that influenced their actions, a deeper understanding of the battle's dynamics emerges.

Moreover, it is crucial to delve into the tactical aspects of the battle. This includes examining the deployment of troops, the utilization of weaponry, and the maneuvering of forces on the battlefield. By analyzing these intricacies, readers can gain insight into the effectiveness of specific tactics and the impact they had on the outcome of the battle.

Another area to explore is the role of leadership during the battle. This involves studying the qualities and decision-making abilities of the commanding officers on both sides. By highlighting their strengths, weaknesses, and the overall impact they had on their respective forces, readers can appreciate the significance of effective leadership in the midst of intense conflict.

Furthermore, it is essential to discuss the human experience of the battle. This includes examining the psychological and emotional toll on the soldiers, as well as the impact on the civilian populations. By acknowledging the personal sacrifices and hardships endured by those involved, readers can develop a more empathetic and holistic understanding of the battle.

Additionally, exploring the aftermath of the battle is crucial for comprehending its historical significance. This involves analyzing the political, social, and economic consequences of the outcome. By examining the ripple effects that followed the battle, readers can appreciate the long-term implications it had on the nations involved, including changes in borders, power dynamics, and the trajectory of the wider conflict. By providing an overview that covers the geopolitical context, strategic objectives, tactical aspects, leadership dynamics, human experience, and aftermath, readers can gain a comprehensive understanding of the battle. It is through a balanced and analytical approach that we can truly appreciate the impact and historical significance of this momentous event.

Significance of the battle

Battles have been pivotal in determining the fate of nations, altering political landscapes, and influencing social, cultural, and economic developments. Understanding the significance of a battle requires an analysis of its military, political, and social aspects, as well as its long-term effects on various spheres of society. In this book, we will delve into the significance of different battles throughout history, exploring key events and their aftermaths, in order to gain a comprehensive understanding of the importance battles have held in shaping our world.

Historical Perspectives:

To fully comprehend the significance of any battle, it is essential to examine the historical context in which it occurred. Battles arise from a complex web of historical events, grievances, alliances, and ambitions. For instance, the Battle of Waterloo in 1815, which marked the end of Napoleon Bonaparte's reign, was not just a clash between two armies. It represented the culmination of years of conflict and power struggles among European countries. By examining the historical backdrop, we can understand how battles become turning points, bringing about decisive changes in history.

Military Significance:

The military significance of a battle lies in its strategic and tactical implications. Battles often require military commanders to demonstrate superior planning, leadership, and use of resources. The outcome of a battle can be determined by a wide range of factors, including training, equipment, technology, terrain, and the morale of troops. The Battle of Stalingrad during World War II serves as a prime example of military significance. The Soviet Union's victory led to a major shift in the balance of power, symbolizing the turning point of the war on the Eastern Front.

Political Impact:

Battles can have far-reaching political consequences, shaping the destiny of nations and leaders. The Battle of Hastings in 1066, for instance, marked the beginning of Norman rule in England, ending the Anglo-Saxon era. It had profound political implications, introducing a new ruling class and altering the social fabric of the country. Battles can also trigger political changes by toppling regimes or sparking revolutions, as seen in the Battle of Yorktown during the American Revolutionary War, which ultimately led to the independence of the United States.

Social and Cultural Changes:

The significance of battles often transcends the realm of warfare, touching the lives of ordinary people and shaping societies. Battles can give rise to social and cultural changes that alter the course of civilization. For example, the Battle of Plassey in 1757 marked a crucial moment in British colonial history, as it laid the foundation for the expansion of the British Empire in India. The subsequent cultural exchange between the British and Indian civilizations brought about lasting social transformations in both societies.

Economic Implications:

Battles can also have profound economic consequences, influencing trade, resource allocation, and economic development. The Battle of Lepanto in 1571, a naval clash between the Holy League and the Ottoman Empire, ensured the control of the Mediterranean Sea for Christian powers. This victory secured crucial trade routes, allowing Western Europe to expand its influence in the Mediterranean and opening up new economic opportunities for European states.

UNDERSTANDING THE SIGNIFICANCE of battles is essential for comprehending the complexities of our history and the forces that have shaped our world. By examining battles through multiple lenses – historical, military, political, social, and economic – we gain insight into the interconnectedness of these aspects and how they have affected different societies. From turning points in history to the emergence of new powers, battles have left indelible imprints on our past, present, and future. By studying their significance, we can appreciate the immense impact that battles have had in shaping our world.

Impact on the outcome of the war

In this exploration of the topic, we will delve into the various aspects that impact the outcome of a war and shed light on the critical factors that determine victory or defeat. By examining a range of historical conflicts across different eras and geographies, we aim to elucidate the important elements that contribute to the final outcome, forging an understanding of how wars are won or lost.

1. Military Strength and Strategy:

One of the fundamental determinants of a war's outcome lies in the military strength and strategy of the opposing factions. The size, training, and equipment of armies, navies, and air forces play crucial roles in shaping the battlefront. Superior weaponry, technological advancements, and military doctrines can provide a significant advantage. Strategic planning, including the selection of battlefields, coordination of forces, and the ability to adapt to evolving circumstances, often differentiates the victorious side from the defeated. Historical examples such as the Battle of Waterloo, where the Duke of Wellington's strategic decisions led to Napoleon's downfall, illustrate the immense significance of military strength and strategy.

2. Leadership and Command:

Effective leadership has a profound impact on the outcome of a war. Successful commanders possess the ability to inspire, motivate, and instill discipline within their troops. They make critical decisions under extreme pressure, while also displaying adaptability and tactical brilliance. Leaders such as General George Washington in the American Revolutionary War or Admiral Horatio Nelson during the Battle of Trafalgar shaped their respective conflicts through their strategic genius, meticulous planning, and exceptional leadership skills. Conversely, weak or inept leadership can prove fatal, leading to confusion, disarray, and ultimately, defeat.

3. Economic Resources and Industrial Capacity:

Another crucial factor that can sway the outcome of a war is the economic resources and industrial capacity at the disposal of a nation. Adequate financial reserves, robust supply lines, and a capable industrial base are vital in sustaining a prolonged conflict. The ability to arm troops, produce munitions, and sustain logistical support determines the staying power of a belligerent. The American Civil War showcased the North's superior industrial capacity, allowing it to outproduce the South and ultimately secure victory. Similarly, the economic strain on Germany during World War I due to a lack of resources played a significant role in its eventual defeat.

4. Technological Advancements:

Technological advancements often revolutionize warfare, altering the balance of power and reshaping the outcome of a conflict. Innovations such as gunpowder in medieval times, rifling in firearms during the American Civil War, and the deployment of tanks and aircraft during World War I have all had profound effects on battles. The successful utilization of new technologies confers advantages such as increased firepower, mobility, and enhanced communication, giving the innovation's progenitors the edge in battle. The impact of technological advancements is undeniable, as seen in the Allied victory during World War II with the introduction of nuclear weapons and the advancements in radar and encryption technology.

5. Morale and Public Support:

The morale and public support of both the military and civilian populations can exert a substantial influence on the outcome of a war. High morale fosters unity, determination, and a willingness to endure hardships. Effective propaganda campaigns, political leadership, and community cohesion all contribute to the maintenance of high morale. Conversely, low morale can lead to desertion, rebellion, and defeat. The morale of the troops involved in the Battle of Stalingrad, for example, played a crucial role in turning the tide against the Nazis, as Soviet soldiers and civilians exhibited unparalleled resilience and determination.

6. Diplomacy and Alliances:

The role of diplomacy and alliances cannot be discounted when evaluating the outcome of a conflict. Successful diplomacy can lead to favorable alliances that provide military, economic, and political support. History is replete with examples where alliances have tipped the scales in favor of a particular side, such as the alliances forged by the Allied powers during both World Wars. Conversely, failed diplomacy or the lack of strategic alliances can leave a nation isolated and vulnerable, potentially resulting in defeat.

UNDERSTANDING THE FACTORS that impact the outcome of a war is instrumental in comprehending the intricacies of historical conflicts and their ramifications. The interplay between military strength and strategy, leadership and command, economic resources and industrial capacity, technological advancements, morale and public support, and diplomacy and alliances all shape the course of war. While no two wars are the same, analyzing these key factors across various conflicts offers valuable insights into the determinants of victory or defeat. By grasping the complexities of war, we can gain a deeper appreciation for the significance of these factors and their implications in shaping the annals of history.

Chapter 6: Sherman's March to the Sea

GENERAL SHERMAN'S MILITARY tactics

One of Sherman's most notable military tactics was his concept of "March to the Sea" during the Atlanta Campaign in 1864. After capturing Atlanta, Sherman embarked on a bold and audacious march towards the coast, systematically destroying all resources, infrastructure, and supplies in his path. This scorched-earth policy aimed to cripple the Confederate war effort by depriving them of food, shelter, and logistical support. By cutting off the South from its supply lines and crippling its economy, Sherman hoped to break the will of the Confederacy and force a surrender.

Sherman's "March to the Sea" was not just a military campaign; it was a psychological warfare strategy. By targeting civilian infrastructure and property, he aimed to demoralize the Southern population and diminish their support for the war. This approach was a departure from traditional military tactics, which focused primarily on engaging enemy armies on the battlefield. Sherman understood the importance of attacking the enemy's will to fight and recognized that the Southern population was not just a bystander but an integral part of the Confederate war effort.

While Sherman's tactics were effective in crippling the Southern economy, they also brought destruction and suffering to many innocent civilians. The deliberate targeting of infrastructure and private property had devastating consequences for the people living in the path of Sherman's army. This aspect of Sherman's military tactics has sparked debate and controversy, with some historians arguing that the tactics bordered on war crimes, while others defend them as a necessary means to bring the war to a swift conclusion.

Another significant aspect of Sherman's military tactics was his concept of "total war." Unlike previous commanders who limited their military operations to targeting enemy armies, Sherman advocated for a comprehensive, all-encompassing approach. He believed that victory could only be achieved by targeting not just the military forces but also the civilian infrastructure and resources that sustained the Confederacy. This concept, while highly controversial, marked a shift in the understanding of warfare and had a profound impact on subsequent military strategies.

Sherman's use of psychological warfare extended beyond the destruction of physical assets. He recognized the importance of perceptions and public opinion in war, particularly in a divided nation like the United States during the Civil War. To this end, he employed the media and played on the fears and insecurities of the Southern population. By projecting an image of an indomitable and relentless force, Sherman further weakened the resolve of the Confederate forces and contributed to their ultimate defeat.

It is important to note that Sherman's military tactics were not limited to his "March to the Sea" and total war approach. His success in the Atlanta Campaign and subsequent campaigns in the Carolinas showcased his exceptional strategic acumen and ability to outmaneuver and outthink his opponents. By constantly keeping the Confederates off-balance and applying relentless pressure, Sherman ensured that they were unable to mount an effective defense, leading to their eventual collapse. Through his "March to the Sea," total war strategy, and innovative use of psychological warfare, Sherman demonstrated a new approach to warfare that aimed to cripple the enemy's infrastructure and demoralize the civilian population. While these tactics were controversial and brought suffering to many innocent civilians, they undoubtedly played a crucial role in securing a Union victory. Sherman's legacy as a military strategist and his contributions to the evolution of warfare continue to be studied and debated by historians to this day.

Destruction of the South

The war had devastated the region, leaving behind a landscape of destruction that mirrored the shattered state of Southern society and economy. In this book, we aim to delve into the factors that contributed to the destruction of the South, shedding light on both the immediate and long-term effects of this period on the region. Through a comprehensive analysis and exploration of historical events and their impact, we hope to provide a clearer understanding of the post-war South, the difficulties it faced, and the evolution it underwent.

From War to Destruction: A Nation Divided

The Civil War was a defining moment in American history, pitting the North against the South in a struggle for political, economic, and social ideologies. The destruction of the South, however, was not solely a result of military defeat but rather a complex interplay of factors. The war's toll can be seen in the physical devastation of Southern cities, towns, and farms, as well as the psychological trauma inflicted on its population. This one will explore the military strategies employed by Union forces, detailing the deliberate targeting of Southern infrastructure, the impact of the blockade, and the widespread displacement of civilians. By examining these events, we gain a deeper understanding of how the destruction unfolded and its immediate consequences for the region.

The Economic Fallout: From Rags to Riches

Beyond the immediate destruction caused by the war, the Southern economy also faced a post-war struggle for survival. The collapse of the plantation system, which had relied on the institution of slavery, led to a profound shift in labor dynamics and disrupted agricultural practices. This one will focus on the challenges faced by former slaveholders, the emergence of sharecropping and tenant farming systems, and the devastation wrought upon the banking and manufacturing sectors. We will explore how these economic changes influenced Southern society, including the emergence of a new class structure and the unequal distribution of wealth. In doing so, we can gain insights into the long-term consequences of the destruction of the South's economy.

Rebuilding a Broken Society: Challenges of Race and Democracy

The Reconstruction era was a time of great hope, with the promise of equality and freedom for all individuals. Yet, the reality of racial tensions and political maneuvering proved to be one of the greatest challenges faced by the war-torn South. This one will delve into the complexities of racial relations during Reconstruction, examining the rise of white supremacy groups, the implementation of Black Codes, and the role of federal legislation and enforcement. We will explore the struggles of African Americans as they sought to secure their civil and political rights amidst a climate of segregation and violence. By understanding the challenges faced by the South in terms of race and democracy, we can better comprehend the lasting impact of this tumultuous period.

The Legacy of Destruction: Southern Identity in Flux

The destruction of the South, both physical and societal, left an indelible mark on the region's identity. This one will examine how the collective memory of the war and the subsequent Reconstruction period shaped Southern identity, emphasizing the emergence of the "Lost Cause" narrative and the glorification of the antebellum South. We will explore the ways in which this narrative influenced art, literature, and popular culture, perpetuating stereotypes and inhibiting reconciliation. Additionally, we will investigate the impact of Confederate monument construction and revisionist attitudes toward the war. By exploring the complexities of Southern identity, we gain a deeper understanding of how the destruction shaped the region for generations to come.

THE RECONSTRUCTION period following the Civil War was a time of immense destruction and profound transformation for the South. From physical devastation to the economic and social upheaval, the challenges faced by the region were formidable. Our exploration of these challenges and their consequences aims to shed light on the complexities of this era, dispelling misconceptions and fostering a deeper understanding of the Southern experience. By addressing the destruction in a professional, academic, and approachable manner, we hope to engage readers and contribute to a more comprehensive understanding of the lasting impact of the Reconstruction period on the South.

Effects on the Confederate morale

One of the most significant factors that eroded Confederate morale was the succession of military setbacks experienced by the southern forces. From the early stages of the war, the Confederacy faced numerous defeats, such as the Battle of Gettysburg and the surrender of Vicksburg. These defeats not only resulted in substantial losses of men and resources but also shattered the confidence of the Confederate soldiers and civilians alike. As news of these defeats spread, it became increasingly difficult to maintain a positive outlook on the war effort. Moreover, these military setbacks often exposed the shortcomings of Confederate leadership, further undermining the perceived effectiveness of their cause.

Alongside the military setbacks, the Confederate morale faced additional challenges due to economic struggles. The Confederacy relied heavily on agriculture, particularly the cotton industry, for revenue. However, the blockade imposed by the Union Navy severely hampered the Confederacy's ability to export its cotton and import necessary supplies. This economic squeeze led to widespread shortages of basic goods, including food, clothing, and medicine. Such scarcity not only heavily affected the civilian population but also had a direct impact on the morale of the soldiers. Witnessing their families and communities suffer from deprivation only added to the growing sense of despair and weariness among the Confederate troops.

Political divisions also played a crucial role in undermining Confederate morale. Throughout the war, there were tensions between Confederate President Jefferson Davis and some state governors, military leaders, and even within the Confederate Congress. These divisions often manifested in disagreements over strategy, resource allocation, and the role of states' rights within the Confederacy. The lack of a unified political front dampened morale and created a sense of uncertainty and doubt. Soldiers and civilians became disillusioned as they witnessed political squabbles impede effective decision-making and hinder the assertive pursuit of victory.

Societal changes during the Civil War also impacted Confederate morale. As the war dragged on, enthusiasm and initial fervor gradually waned among some segments of the southern population. Initially, many believed that the Confederacy would quickly achieve independence, and excitement fueled popular support for the cause. However, as the human cost became apparent, and as the war presented increasingly gruesome realities, fatigue and war-weariness set in. Confederate morale struggled to withstand the lengthy conflict, and dissent and desertion became more prevalent. The war's physical and psychological toll on soldiers and civilians alike contributed to a decline in overall commitment and enthusiasm, further weakening Confederate morale. Military setbacks, economic struggles, political divisions, and societal changes all played a role in eroding the resolve of the Confederate forces. These factors created a sense of disillusionment, despair, and weariness among soldiers and civilians alike. However, it is important to note that despite these challenges, many Confederates remained fiercely committed to their cause until the very end. Understanding the complexities of Confederate morale provides crucial insights into the ultimate defeat of the Confederacy and the lasting impact of the Civil War on American society.

Chapter 7: Reconstruction Era

EFFORTS TO REUNITE the nation

One of the key factors in successful nation reunification efforts is open and inclusive dialogue. Building bridges between different factions, communities, or regions is crucial to understanding the roots of division and finding common ground. This often involves establishing platforms for dialogue, such as truth and reconciliation commissions or community forums, where all voices are heard and respected. Facilitated discussions allow grievances to be aired, misconceptions to be corrected, and empathy to be fostered. By creating space for dialogue, nations can work towards addressing historical injustices, exploring different perspectives, and finding shared values that can serve as a foundation for unity.

Education and awareness play integral roles in reuniting a nation. By acknowledging and teaching a comprehensive and accurate history of events that led to division, societies can develop a greater sense of understanding and empathy. This education should not only focus on the conflicts themselves but also on the shared cultural heritage and values that bind people together. Through education, people can begin to challenge ingrained stereotypes, prejudices, and biases that perpetuate division. By promoting a shared narrative with diverse perspectives, nations can overcome historical wounds and foster a sense of belonging and national identity that transcends divisions.

Another important aspect of reuniting a nation is reconciliation and healing. Acknowledging past wrongs and ensuring that justice is served is essential for moving forward. This may involve reparations for victims, the establishment of truth and justice mechanisms, and public apologies. Reconciliation requires open and honest dialogue, compassion, and a commitment to learning from the mistakes of the past. By providing avenues for healing, nations can promote a culture of forgiveness and empathy, allowing individuals and communities to address trauma and rebuild their lives.

CIVIL WAR POLITICS: THE DIVIDED NATION AND ITS LEADERS

Economic development is often a catalyst for bringing people from different parts of a divided nation together. By creating opportunities for employment, business, and investment, nations can bridge socioeconomic gaps and alleviate tensions. Infrastructure projects, job creation initiatives, and equitable distribution of resources can help equalize opportunities and improve living conditions for all citizens. Economic development also provides a platform for collaboration and cooperation, as people from different backgrounds work together towards a common goal. This shared experience can foster a sense of belonging and unity, as individuals realize their interconnectedness and shared destiny.

Building trust and social cohesion is a fundamental component of reunification efforts. Trust is often damaged during times of conflict or division, and it must be rebuilt through deliberate actions and policies. This can involve establishing institutions and mechanisms that promote transparency, accountability, and equal opportunities. It may also include promoting intergroup interactions, cultural exchange programs, and initiatives that promote social integration. By actively encouraging cross-cultural understanding and creating spaces for interaction, nations can break down prejudices and foster a sense of national unity.

Leadership plays a pivotal role in reunification efforts. Effective leaders have the ability to bring people together, inspire change, and overcome deep divisions. They must embody the values of inclusivity, empathy, and integrity. Through their actions and rhetoric, leaders can set the tone for a united nation, promoting reconciliation and cooperation. Leadership should also be diverse and representative, reflecting the plurality of the nation and ensuring that all voices are heard and considered. By prioritizing the interests of the entire nation over partisan or divisive agendas, leaders can rally people around a common vision.

While the path to reunification is often challenging and complex, history has shown time and again that it is possible to overcome deep divisions and build a nation that is stronger and more united. By fostering open dialogue, promoting education and awareness, facilitating reconciliation and healing, fostering economic development, building trust and social cohesion, and providing strong leadership, nations can overcome their differences and move towards a brighter, more unified future. This book will illuminate the various strategies and approaches used throughout history and provide valuable insights for those seeking to bring people together and heal the wounds of division.

Reconstruction policies

To truly grasp the importance of Reconstruction policies, it is imperative to first understand the context in which they emerged. The American Civil War, fought from 1861 to 1865, tore the nation apart, leaving behind a fractured society and a devastated economy. The defeat of the Confederacy marked a turning point, as the United States now faced the daunting task of reuniting a divided nation, abolishing slavery, and integrating millions of newly freed African Americans into society.

Reconstruction policies sought to address these immense challenges through a variety of measures. One of the key objectives was to ensure the rights and freedoms of the formerly enslaved population. The Thirteenth, Fourteenth, and Fifteenth Amendments to the United States Constitution were instrumental in achieving this goal. The Thirteenth Amendment, ratified in 1865, abolished slavery throughout the country, extinguishing the institution that had been at the heart of the conflict. The Fourteenth Amendment, adopted in 1868, granted citizenship to all persons born or naturalized in the United States, and it guaranteed equal protection under the law. In brief, the Fifteenth Amendment, ratified in 1870, safeguarded the right to vote for African American men.

These constitutional amendments formed the legal foundation for Reconstruction policies, but their enforcement faced significant obstacles. The Southern states, which had seceded from the Union and formed the Confederacy, resisted the changes brought about by Reconstruction. They implemented a range of discriminatory practices, such as poll taxes, literacy tests, and violent acts of intimidation, aimed at suppressing the political power of African Americans. In response, the federal government took various measures to ensure compliance, including the deployment of troops in the South.

The economic dimension of Reconstruction policies was also crucial. The Civil War had ravaged the Southern economy, and its agriculture-based society was in ruins. To address this, the federal government initiated programs to rebuild infrastructure, promote industrial development, and provide aid to the destitute. The Freedmen's Bureau, established in 1865, played a critical role by providing assistance to the newly freed African Americans, including education, healthcare, and employment opportunities. These efforts aimed to not only alleviate the suffering caused by the war but also foster economic growth in the South.

However, Reconstruction policies faced fierce opposition from various sectors of society. Many white Southerners, resentful of their defeat in the Civil War and the abolition of slavery, sought to preserve their social and economic dominance over African Americans. They resorted to violence, forming organizations like the Ku Klux Klan, to intimidate and suppress the newly gained rights of African Americans. The federal government struggled to effectively combat this resistance, and as a result, the promises of Reconstruction fell short in many areas.

By the late 1870s, Reconstruction began to lose momentum, and its policies were gradually abandoned. This shift was influenced by a variety of factors, including political compromises, fatigue with the contentious issues of race, and economic challenges. The ensuing decades witnessed the rise of Jim Crow laws, which institutionalized racial segregation and further marginalized African Americans. They aimed to rebuild a nation torn apart by civil war, eradicate the institution of slavery, and secure the rights of newly freed African Americans. While these policies achieved significant milestones, such as the abolition of slavery and the granting of citizenship and voting rights, they faced fierce opposition and ultimately fell short of their lofty objectives. Nevertheless, Reconstruction remains a testament to the resilience and determination of a nation striving to redefine itself and forge a more inclusive and just society.

Challenges faced by the reunited nation

These challenges are not merely confined to the political or economic realms but extend to social, cultural, and psychological dimensions as well. Reuniting a nation is a complex task that requires delicate balance and meticulous planning. This book aims to explore and shed light on the challenges faced by a reunited nation and offer insights into the processes, strategies, and potential solutions that can pave the way for a successful and sustainable future.

Healing Wounds and Reconciliation:

One of the foremost challenges confronting a reunited nation is the process of healing deep-rooted wounds and fostering reconciliation among its citizens. The division that once plagued the nation has invariably left scars in the collective memory and psyche of the people. Acknowledgment of past grievances, promoting dialogue, and creating platforms for truth and reconciliation commissions are crucial in paving the way for healing and rebuilding trust. By addressing these unresolved issues, the wounds can gradually heal, and the nation can move forward together.

Economic Integration:

Reunification often poses unique challenges to the economic landscape of a nation. Integration of economic systems, markets, and industries can be complex and intricate. Disparities in wealth, resources, and infrastructural development between the formerly divided regions may hinder the process of economic integration. To overcome these challenges, implementing fair policies, providing financial support, and investing in infrastructure in the previously disadvantaged regions can help bridge the gap, foster economic equality, and create a stronger and more cohesive nation.

Social and Cultural Identity:

Cultural and social unity is imperative for the stability and progress of a reunited nation. The reunification of a nation often brings together diverse cultural backgrounds, languages, customs, and values. Preserving cultural diversity while forging a harmonious identity is a multifaceted challenge. Encouraging cultural exchange, supporting inclusive policies, and investing in education are vital steps towards fostering a shared national identity without eradicating individual cultural expressions.

Overcoming Political Polarization:

Reunification often exacerbates existing political divisions and creates new fault lines within the nation's political landscape. Overcoming political polarization is critical to establish a unified vision and coherent governance. Promoting dialogue, building consensus, and investing in political education and awareness can facilitate the bridging of political divides. Emphasizing inclusivity and enhancing democratic institutions will enable the reunified nation to navigate through the challenges that arise from political differences.

Infrastructure Development:

Reuniting a nation also means addressing disparities in infrastructure development between the formerly divided regions. Neglected or poorly developed infrastructure can impede economic growth, social cohesion, and regional equality. This challenge can be overcome by investing in transport networks, communication systems, energy grids, and urban planning that prioritize equitable distribution. A well-connected and developed infrastructure network will facilitate the flow of goods, services, and ideas, fostering unity and integration.

Education and Re-Education:

Education plays a critical role in shaping the future of a reunified nation. It is imperative to foster an inclusive and progressive education system that acknowledges all aspects of the nation's history. Addressing biases, promoting critical thinking, and teaching empathy will equip young generations with the skills necessary to overcome differences and contribute to a united society. Re-educating adults and consciously reshaping societal attitudes through educational initiatives will further support the unity and progress of the nation.

REUNIFICATION IS A challenging journey that demands collective commitment, perseverance, and a shared vision. By effectively addressing the challenges discussed in this book, a reunited nation can embark on a path of restoration, progress, and prosperity. Healing wounds, fostering reconciliation, promoting economic integration, embracing diverse cultural identities, overcoming political polarization, and prioritizing infrastructure and education are key steps towards building a cohesive and flourishing nation. The challenges may be considerable, but with dedication and collective effort, a reunified nation can rise above its past divisions and forge a brighter future for all.

Chapter 8: The Legacy of the Civil War

LONG-TERM IMPACT OF the war

One of the most apparent and immediate consequences of war is the physical destruction it wreaks on societies. Cities reduced to rubble, infrastructure razed to the ground, and valuable resources depleted or wasted contribute to significant economic and social setbacks. Rebuilding shattered communities, repairing infrastructure, and revitalizing economies can take decades, if not longer. The financial burden of war's aftermath weighs heavily on nations, diverting resources that could have been invested in development and progress towards healing and recovery.

Beyond the physical damage, war leaves a trail of emotional and psychological scars that permeate societies for generations. Soldiers returning from the battlefield often suffer from post-traumatic stress disorder (PTSD), anxiety, and depression. Their families and loved ones also bear the burden of these mental health challenges. Additionally, civilians caught in the crossfire or displaced from their homes face their own share of trauma and displacement. The psychological toll of war is far-reaching, affecting not only individuals directly involved but also permeating entire communities. Addressing and healing these wounds requires long-term investment in mental health services, support networks, and awareness campaigns.

War also has a profound impact on social structures and relationships within societies. In times of conflict, social cohesion often fractures along the lines of race, ethnicity, religion, or political affiliation, creating deep divisions and fueling future conflicts. This fragmentation can hinder social progress and impede the formation of inclusive and harmonious communities. Rebuilding social trust, fostering understanding, and promoting reconciliation are essential ingredients for long-term stability and peace.

Moreover, the long-term impact of war extends beyond national borders, rippling through the international community. Wars often result in geopolitical shifts, redrawing boundaries and altering power dynamics. The consequences of these shifts can be felt for decades as new alliances form, old rivalries intensify, and global power centers realign. The aftermath of war can also give rise to transnational issues, including refugee crises, mass migration, and the spread of terrorism. Addressing these challenges requires international cooperation, diplomacy, and a concerted effort to learn from the lessons of the past in order to build a more peaceful future.

In the wake of war, there is a need for reconciliation and justice. Transitional justice mechanisms, such as truth commissions, tribunals, and reparations processes, are crucial for acknowledging past atrocities, facilitating healing, and fostering a sense of accountability. These measures play a vital role in preventing the reemergence of conflict and ensuring a future where the mistakes of the past are not repeated.

However, it is important to acknowledge that the long-term impact of war is not exclusively negative. While wars bring devastation and suffering, they can also serve as catalysts for social change, innovation, and resilience. Through adversity, communities often find strength, develop resilience, and unite in the face of hardship. Scientific and technological advancements are often born out of wartime necessity, pushing the boundaries of human knowledge and innovation. Furthermore, conflicts can create opportunities for reevaluation and restructuring, leading to the implementation of fairer and more inclusive political and social systems. It leaves lasting scars on individuals, societies, and the global community. The physical destruction, psychological trauma, social divisions, and geopolitical shifts caused by war demand a comprehensive and sustained response. Rebuilding, healing, and working towards a more peaceful future require not only the commitment of nations and governments but also the collective efforts of individuals, communities, and international organizations. By recognizing the far-reaching consequences of war, we can strive towards a world where conflict is minimized and the possibility of a lasting peace becomes a reality.

Changes in American society

One of the most noticeable changes in American society is the evolution of gender roles and the pursuit of gender equality. From the early years of the Republic to the present day, the status and roles of women have undergone profound transformations. Women's suffrage, achieved in 1920 with the ratification of the 19th Amendment, marked a turning point in the recognition of women's rights. However, the struggle for gender equality did not end there. Throughout the 20th century, women have challenged traditional gender roles and fought for access to education, career opportunities, and reproductive rights. The feminist movement of the 1960s and 1970s played a crucial role in advancing these causes, leading to increased female representation in the workforce and political arena. Today, although progress has been made, gender inequalities persist. Issues such as the gender pay gap, underrepresentation of women in leadership positions, and gender-based violence remain prevalent. In order to achieve true equality, ongoing efforts are needed at societal, institutional, and individual levels.

Another significant shift in American society is the quest for racial equality. The United States has a complex history when it comes to race, with slavery and racial discrimination being deeply ingrained in its past. However, the civil rights movement of the 1950s and 1960s brought about monumental changes in this regard. Led by influential figures such as Martin Luther King Jr., this movement fought for the recognition of African Americans' rights, including the right to vote, equal education, and an end to segregation. The passage of landmark legislation, such as the Civil Rights Act of 1964 and the Voting Rights Act of 1965, helped dismantle legal barriers to equality. These groundbreaking changes laid the foundation for greater inclusion and diversity in American society. Nevertheless, racial disparities persist in areas such as education, criminal justice, and economic opportunities. The Black Lives Matter movement, born in response to police brutality and systemic racism, has brought renewed attention to these issues in recent years. Addressing structural inequalities, fostering inclusivity, and dismantling systemic racism are ongoing challenges that must be confronted to further advance racial equality.

Cultural diversity is another vital aspect of American society that has seen significant changes over time. The United States is a melting pot of cultures, shaped by waves of immigration throughout its history. From the early European settlers to more recent arrivals from Asia, Latin America, and Africa, these diverse groups have contributed to the nation's rich tapestry. However, the perception and treatment of immigrants have varied throughout different periods. The early 20th century witnessed restrictive immigration policies, such as the Chinese Exclusion Act and the quotas set by the Immigration Act of 1924. Contrastingly, the Immigration and Nationality Act of 1965 ushered in a new era, abolishing national origin quotas and prioritizing family reunification and skilled immigrants. These changes, along with subsequent immigration reforms, have led to a more diverse and multicultural society. Today, immigrants play a vital role in various sectors of the economy, enriching American culture with their traditions, languages, and perspectives. However, debates surrounding immigration policies and cultural assimilation persist, underscoring the ongoing tensions and challenges associated with cultural diversity in American society. Through examining the transformations in gender roles, racial equality, and cultural diversity, we gain insights into the ongoing journey of American society toward greater inclusivity and equality. Achieving true gender equality, eradicating racial disparities, and embracing cultural diversity remain ongoing challenges that require continuous efforts from individuals, communities, and institutions. By understanding and addressing these issues, we can foster a society that celebrates the diverse experiences and aspirations of all its members, thus realizing the true ideals and potential of the United States of America.

Lessons learned from the conflict

Throughout the ages, societies and nations have borne witness to wars, revolutions, and internal tensions that have shaped their destiny. From the bloody battlefields of ancient civilizations to the ideological clashes of the modern era, conflicts have left their mark on humanity. However, in the aftermath of these tumultuous periods, valuable lessons have been learned. By examining these lessons through both an academic and practical lens, we can understand the path towards a more peaceful coexistence and the vital importance of compassionate diplomacy.

1. Understanding the Root Causes:

The first lesson we can glean from conflicts is the importance of understanding their root causes. Conflict rarely arises out of thin air but is often deeply rooted in social, political, economic, or cultural dynamics. By delving into these causes, we gain a more comprehensive awareness of the underlying issues fueling conflict. Armed with this knowledge, we can work towards addressing these grievances, thereby paving the way for a more harmonious society. Education, cross-cultural dialogue, and inclusive governance are just a few of the avenues we can employ to understand the root causes and tackle them head-on.

2. The Power of Effective Communication:

Miscommunication and misunderstanding are often at the heart of conflicts. The second lesson we learn entails the power of effective communication in preventing and resolving disputes. During conflicts, tensions can run high, and emotions may cloud rationality. In these situations, it is crucial to foster open, honest, and respectful dialogue. By encouraging active listening and empathy, we can build bridges of understanding and find common ground amidst differences. In conflict resolution, diplomacy is a powerful tool that emphasizes communication, negotiation, and compromise to dissolve animosity and foster mutual respect.

3. Promoting Empathy and Compassion:

Empathy and compassion play pivotal roles in both preventing conflicts and healing their scars. When societies and individuals cultivate these qualities, they embrace a mindset that seeks to understand the perspectives and experiences of others. By acknowledging the multidimensionality of conflicts, we can move beyond rigid divides and formulate win-win solutions. Encouraging empathy through education, storytelling, and community engagement allows us to break free from the cycle of violence and forge lasting peace based on mutual understanding and respect.

4. The Art of Forgiveness and Healing:

Resolution and reconciliation often necessitate forgiveness and healing. The fourth lesson learned from conflicts is the transformative power of forgiveness. While forgiving may seem an arduous or even impossible task, it bestows forgiveness on both the individual and society as a whole. Forgiveness does not mean forgetting; rather, it involves acknowledging the past while striving for a better future. Through truth-telling mechanisms, memorialization efforts, and justice systems that prioritize reparations over revenge, societies can heal their wounds, restore trust, and move towards a more inclusive society that embraces peace and social harmony.

5. Long-Term Investment in Social Justice:

Conflict can highlight the underlying social injustices that breed resentment and unrest. The final lesson we explore is the importance of addressing these injustices as a means to prevent future conflicts. By understanding the systemic inequalities that perpetuate social divisions, societies can strive for equity, human rights, and inclusive governance structures. Investing in education, healthcare, access to justice, and economic opportunities for all members of society creates a foundation for sustainable peace. Working towards eliminating discrimination, poverty, and exclusion helps build a just society where everyone has an equal chance to thrive.

THE LESSONS LEARNED from past conflicts provide a roadmap for fostering peace, reconciliation, and social cohesion. By understanding the root causes, promoting effective communication, nurturing empathy and compassion, embracing forgiveness, and investing in social justice, societies can extricate themselves from the cycle of violence and forge a brighter and more harmonious future. Lessons from the conflict teach us that conflict resolution is an active endeavor that requires concerted efforts from individuals, communities, and nations. It is through these lessons and a deep commitment to peaceful coexistence that we can forge a world where conflict becomes the exception, not the norm.

Chapter 9: Key Figures of the Civil War

PROFILES OF IMPORTANT leaders

These leaders have demonstrated remarkable qualities such as vision, charisma, determination, and the ability to inspire others. In this book, we will explore the profiles of some of the most important leaders in history, analyzing their leadership styles, achievements, and the lessons we can derive from their experiences. By learning about these influential figures, we can gain valuable insights into effective leadership and also gain inspiration for our own personal and professional journeys.

Abraham Lincoln – A Beacon of Moral Leadership

Abraham Lincoln, the 16th President of the United States, is widely regarded as one of the greatest leaders in American history. His unwavering commitment to justice, equality, and integrity during one of the nation's most turbulent times played a pivotal role in shaping the future of the nation. Lincoln's leadership style was characterized by his ability to empathize with others, his willingness to listen to diverse perspectives, and his firm belief in the power of moral principles. His approach to leadership, rooted in moral values and a deep sense of duty, serves as a timeless example of leadership by example. The story of Lincoln's leadership reminds us of the importance of staying true to our values, even in the face of adversity, and the profound impact a leader can have on society by prioritizing the greater good.

Winston Churchill - Courageous Leadership in Times of Crisis

Sir Winston Churchill, the British Prime Minister during World War II, exemplifies the qualities of a true leader in times of crisis. With his indomitable spirit, wit, and rhetoric, he united the British people, inspiring them to persevere through the darkest days of the war. Churchill's leadership style was characterized by his ability to make tough decisions, communicate effectively, and motivate his followers through his unwavering determination. His ability to confront challenges head-on, learn from failures, and maintain unwavering optimism is a valuable lesson for leaders facing tumultuous times. Churchill's leadership legacy demonstrates that true leaders rise above adversity, instill hope in others, and act decisively when circumstances demand it.

Mahatma Gandhi - An Icon of Nonviolent Leadership

Mahatma Gandhi, the leader of India's struggle for independence, is renowned for his philosophy of nonviolence and his unwavering commitment to justice. Gandhi adopted a unique leadership approach based on personal ethics, nonviolent resistance, and the power of self-sacrifice. He believed in the capacity of individuals to effect social change through peaceful means. Gandhi's leadership style was characterized by his ability to influence others through his simple lifestyle, empathetic nature, and unwavering dedication to his principles. He inspired millions to rise against injustice and taught the world that leadership is not about wielding power but rather about serving others and the greater good. Gandhi's leadership philosophy serves as a guiding light for leaders seeking to enact positive change in their communities through peaceful means.

Nelson Mandela - Transformational Leadership for a New South Africa

Nelson Mandela, South Africa's first black President, is considered one of the most influential leaders of the 20th century. Mandela's extraordinary journey from prisoner to president symbolizes his unwavering commitment to justice, reconciliation, and equality. Mandela's leadership style was characterized by his ability to inspire, unite, and transform a divided nation. He emphasized the importance of forgiveness, reconciliation, and inclusivity, setting an example for leaders facing societal divisions. Mandela's story teaches us the importance of leading with empathy, embracing diversity, and steering change through dialogue and understanding. He proved that true leadership lies in the ability to rise above personal grievances and work towards a collective vision of a better future.

THE PROFILES OF THESE important leaders offer us invaluable insights into the qualities, skills, and approaches that define effective leadership. From Abraham Lincoln's moral stewardship to Winston Churchill's resolve in times of crisis, Mahatma Gandhi's commitment to nonviolence to Nelson Mandela's transformative leadership, their legacies continue to inspire and guide leaders across generations. As we explore their stories, we are reminded that leadership is not merely about power and authority but rather about integrity, vision, empathy, and the ability to inspire others to achieve shared goals. By understanding these leaders' strengths and weaknesses, we can learn from their experiences, adapt their leadership principles to our own contexts, and strive to make a positive impact on the world around us.

Contributions to the war effort

One of the most visible and impactful contributions individuals can make to the war effort is through military service. As conflicts erupt, nations call upon their citizens to join the armed forces and defend their homeland. Men and women from all walks of life willingly enlist or are conscripted to serve on the front lines. They undergo rigorous training to equip themselves with the necessary skills and knowledge to face the challenges of war. These brave soldiers exhibit tremendous courage and self-sacrifice as they face the unknown, risking their lives to protect their nation and its ideals.

While military service usually takes center stage in wartime narratives, it is crucial to acknowledge the immense contributions made on the home front. The civilian population plays a pivotal role in supporting the military and sustaining the war effort. On the home front, individuals engage in activities such as working in factories, producing essential war materials, growing food, and rendering various services. These contributions on the home front are indispensable in maintaining the logistics and supply chains necessary for armed forces to operate effectively. The collective efforts of civilians working in tandem with the military create a synergistic effect that enhances the overall strength of a nation at war.

In addition to individual efforts, communities come together to contribute to the war effort on a broader scale. Community-based organizations are often at the forefront of organizing and mobilizing resources to support the armed forces and their families. These organizations establish networks of volunteers who assist in various ways, such as organizing fundraisers, providing medical aid, or offering emotional support. By pooling their resources and talents, communities strengthen the bonds of solidarity and create a supportive environment for those directly impacted by war.

Moreover, institutions, both public and private, play a vital role in contributing to the war effort. Government bodies allocate resources and formulate policies to ensure the smooth functioning of collective defense. They establish and enforce conscription laws, rationing systems, and other measures to ensure the equitable distribution of necessities during times of scarcity. Private institutions, including businesses and corporations, reorient their production towards meeting the demands of wartime necessities. The industrial sector becomes a critical cog in the war machine, producing weapons, vehicles, and other essential supplies for the military. These institutional contributions highlight the interconnectedness of various sectors within a nation during war and demonstrate the collective commitment to achieving success.

The contributions made during times of war have a lasting impact that extends far beyond the conflict itself. The legacy of these efforts shapes the trajectory of nations and societies long after the cessation of hostilities. The skills gained through military service, such as leadership, discipline, and resilience, often prove invaluable in the post-war period. Similarly, the industrial advancements made during wartime production can lead to technological innovations and economic growth in peacetime. Communities that come together during wartime often continue to forge strong social bonds and civic engagement that endure for generations. The contributions to the war effort form a tapestry of experiences and influences that shape the values, identities, and collective memory of a nation. Whether through military service, home front efforts, community mobilization, or institutional support, each contribution is a piece of a larger puzzle that enables a nation to overcome the challenges of war. The impacts of these contributions extend far beyond the battlefield, shaping societies, economies, and the collective memories of nations for years to come. Recognizing and appreciating these contributions not only honors the sacrifices made during war but also provides valuable insights into resilience, unity, and the indomitable spirit of humanity.

Legacy of their actions

However, amidst the chaos, it becomes imperative to pause and reflect on the profound impact our actions can have on society, our loved ones, and future generations. This exploration of our legacy delves into the power we possess as individuals to shape a better world, leaving behind a lasting impression that transcends time. As we unravel the intricacies of our legacy, we discover not only the importance of our actions but also the transformative potential they hold.

The Significance of Our Actions

Our actions, no matter how seemingly insignificant, possess within them the ability to ripple through the fabric of society and leave an indelible impression. Every decision we make, every word we speak, and every deed we perform carries weight. Acknowledging this profound significance empowers us to approach our endeavors with responsibility and care. By recognizing the potential of our acts, we take a step towards creating a legacy worthy of admiration and respect.

Building a Life of Purpose

At the heart of creating a lasting legacy lies the pursuit of purpose. Discovering and nurturing our passions and aligning them with our actions allows us to lead a life driven by meaning and fulfillment. By actively engaging in endeavors that resonate deep within us, we not only leave behind an impactful legacy but also inspire others to follow suit. Building a life of purpose initiates a ripple effect that can cascade through generations, nurturing a culture of purpose-driven acts.

The Butterfly Effect

Often, we underestimate the power of our actions and fail to grasp the interconnectedness of the world. The butterfly effect, popularized by chaos theory, teaches us that even the most inconsequential action can lead to unforeseen consequences. From simply lending a helping hand to making a small positive change in our immediate surroundings, we have the potential to ignite a wave of transformation. Understanding the butterfly effect implores us to be cognizant of our actions and actively seek opportunities to positively impact those around us.

Cultivating Empathy and Compassion

To truly leave a profound and positive legacy, we need to cultivate empathy and compassion in our interactions with others. By trying to understand the perspectives and emotions of those around us, we create an encompassing environment of love, support, and respect. From acts of kindness towards strangers to fostering deeper connections with loved ones, our ability to empathize and show compassion amplifies the far-reaching impact of our actions, shaping a legacy founded on care and understanding.

Transformation Through Giving Back

One of the most tangible ways we can mold our legacy is through giving back. Whether through charitable donations, volunteering our time and skills, or mentoring those in need, acts of altruism significantly contribute to the betterment of society. The opportunity to leave behind a legacy that supports and uplifts others is unparalleled. By investing our resources, expertise, and compassion in the service of those less fortunate, we sow seeds of change that reverberate through time.

Inspiring Future Generations

Our actions extend beyond the present moment; they shape the worldview and values of future generations. Through the power of example, we inspire others to adopt the positive aspects of our legacy, fueling a collective desire to make the world a better place. By sharing our stories, lessons, and experiences, we create a legacy that transcends our physical presence, ensuring the continuation of our impact long after we are gone.

THE LEGACY WE FORGE through our actions has the potential to transform lives, communities, and the world at large. By embracing the significance of our deeds and consciously striving for a purpose-driven existence, we become active contributors to a legacy of significance and positive change. Through empathy, compassion, and generosity, we uplift and inspire those around us, setting in motion a ripple effect that surpasses the passage of time. Let us remember that every action, no matter how small, carries the power to shape a legacy that leaves an enduring mark on our world.

Chapter 10: The Road to Reconciliation

EFFORTS TO HEAL THE nation

One of the most fundamental aspects of healing a nation lies in promoting open and respectful dialogue. Genuine conversations that take place in an environment of mutual understanding and empathy can serve as a powerful catalyst for healing wounds and bridging divides. Engaging in dialogue allows individuals to express their concerns, frustrations, and fears while providing an opportunity for others to listen and validate these experiences. It is crucial to emphasize that in these conversations, the goal should not be to win arguments or impose perspectives, but rather to create an environment conducive to finding common ground. By actively listening and considering multiple viewpoints, society can find ways to address grievances and work towards collective solutions.

Furthermore, efforts to heal the nation require acknowledging and learning from the mistakes or injustices of the past. Many nations have suffered from a history marred by discrimination, violence, or systematic oppression. To build a better future, it is imperative to confront the ghosts of the past head-on and engage in a process of historical reckoning. This involves acknowledging the injustices committed, understanding their impact, and seeking to redress the grievances of affected communities. Taking lessons from countries such as South Africa's Truth and Reconciliation Commission, where victims and perpetrators engaged in a dialogue aimed at healing, forgiveness, and moving forward, can provide a framework for other nations to follow.

Education also plays a central role in healing a divided nation. It is through education that ignorance can be dispelled, prejudices challenged, and understanding fostered. Educational institutions have a responsibility to ensure that their curricula promote inclusivity, diversity, and critical thinking. By teaching history that reflects multiple perspectives, encouraging dialogue between students of different backgrounds, and fostering empathy and understanding, schools can become vehicles for positive social change. Education should extend beyond the classroom, reaching out to communities and providing opportunities for lifelong learning. Providing inclusive education that addresses the diverse needs of all learners, regardless of socioeconomic status or cultural background, is paramount for healing the nation and nurturing future generations.

In addition to dialogue, historical reckoning, and education, efforts to heal the nation must include concrete actions to address systemic inequalities and promote social justice. The divisions that exist within a society are often rooted in disparities in wealth, access to opportunities, and representation. Therefore, addressing these structural inequities is crucial for any healing process to be meaningful and lasting. Governments and institutions should commit to policies that aim to level the playing field, creating equal access to quality education, healthcare, and job opportunities. Moreover, fostering diversity and representation in decision-making positions can ensure that marginalized voices are heard and their concerns addressed. By empowering the most vulnerable members of society, a foundation can be laid for a more equitable and cohesive nation.

The media also holds a crucial role in efforts to heal the nation. In recent times, media platforms have been instrumental in amplifying divisive voices and perpetuating polarization. However, the media can also become a powerful tool for healing and reconciliation if used responsibly. Journalists and media organizations should strive for accuracy, fairness, and an objective portrayal of different perspectives. Sensationalism, fueling conflicts, or promoting misinformation should be replaced with a commitment to ethical reporting that promotes understanding and empathy. Furthermore, promoting diverse voices in the media landscape can help counter the homogeneity of narratives and facilitate a more nuanced understanding of complex social issues.

To culminate, healing the nation requires the active participation of individuals and communities. Each person has the capacity to contribute to the healing process through their actions, words, and relationships. Acts of kindness, empathy, and bridge-building can create a ripple effect that fosters unity and understanding. Engaging with people from different backgrounds, challenging one's own biases, and seeking to understand different perspectives are essential in this endeavor. Healing a nation is a collective responsibility that requires individuals to move beyond their own echo chambers and find common ground with fellow citizens. It requires fostering open dialogue, confronting historical injustices, promoting inclusive education, addressing systemic inequalities, responsible media practices, and the active engagement of citizens. By committing to these strategies, nations can take significant steps towards healing, unity, and a more inclusive future. We hope that this book will serve as a guide and a source of inspiration for those seeking to contribute to the collective healing of their nations and create a more harmonious and equitable world.

Reunification of the country

Throughout history, many countries have experienced the challenges and rewards of reunification. One of the most notable examples is the reunification of Germany. Following decades of division during the Cold War, East and West Germany embarked on a journey of reunification in 1990. This reunification process was not without difficulties, as it required tackling economic disparities, political integration, and even addressing traumatic historical events. However, through a combination of diplomacy, compromise, and determination, Germany successfully reunited, leading to a stronger and more prosperous nation.

The process of reunifying a country is multifaceted and often begins with the recognition and acknowledgement of the existing divisions. It is crucial for the citizens of the respective regions to understand the reasons behind the separation and the potential benefits of reunification. This involves open and empathetic dialogue, educating the population about the shared history, and dispelling any misconceptions or fears that may hinder the reunification process. Building trust and fostering a sense of shared purpose amongst the citizens is of utmost importance in order to achieve a successful reunification.

Political reconciliation and integration play a vital role in the reunification process. The existing political systems in the separate regions might differ significantly, which can lead to challenges in harmonizing laws, policies, and governance structures. It is essential to involve representatives from each region in the decision-making process, ensuring their voices are heard and that their concerns are addressed. A comprehensive plan that outlines the steps towards reunification, including the establishment of a transitional government or interim measures, can help create a sense of stability and continuity during this transformative period.

Economic reunification poses its own set of challenges, as there are often significant disparities in economic development between the divided regions. Addressing these inequities requires a comprehensive strategy aimed at fostering economic growth, job creation, and resource redistribution. Investments in infrastructure, education, and technology can help bridge the economic gap, ensuring that all citizens benefit from the reunification process. Additionally, promoting trade and cooperation between the previously separate regions can lead to increased economic opportunities and mutually beneficial partnerships.

Social and cultural aspects also need to be considered during the reunification process. Differences in language, traditions, and values may have developed during the period of separation, and the reunification journey provides an opportunity to foster understanding and preserve cultural diversity. Encouraging cultural exchanges, promoting tolerance, and celebrating shared traditions can help to bridge social divisions and create a sense of unity and belonging among the citizens of the reunited country. Education and public awareness initiatives can also play a crucial role in promoting inclusivity and fostering a shared national identity.

Reunification is a journey that requires time, patience, and commitment from all parties involved. It is important to manage expectations and recognize that the process may have its setbacks and challenges. However, throughout history, successful reunifications have shown that the rewards of unity far outweigh the difficulties faced along the way. Reunification brings about a sense of national pride, enhanced diplomatic standing, increased economic opportunities, and a newfound sense of belonging for the citizens of the reunited country. The examples of Germany and other countries that have experienced this journey show that despite the challenges, reunification can lead to a stronger, more prosperous, and united nation. By addressing political, economic, social, and cultural divisions, countries can forge a path towards unity, fostering a sense of national identity and ensuring that all citizens benefit from the process. Reunification offers an opportunity to heal past wounds, build bridges between communities, and create a brighter future for generations to come.

Chapter 11: The Role of Women in the Civil War

WOMEN'S CONTRIBUTIONS to the war effort

However, it is crucial to recognize and honor the invaluable role that women played during times of conflict, as their efforts shaped the course of history and pushed societal boundaries. From the home front to the battle lines, women took on various roles that challenged gender norms and proved their resilience, resourcefulness, and dedication in the face of adversity. This discourse aims to shed light on the remarkable accomplishments of women during war periods, celebrate their indomitable spirit, and promote a comprehensive understanding of their multifaceted contributions.

The Emergence of Women in Unconventional Roles

In times of war, the traditional roles assigned to women underwent a remarkable transformation, as the need for manpower pushed society to redefine gender divisions. As men left home to fight on the frontlines, women found themselves thrust into previously male-dominated spheres of employment, such as factories, munitions plants, and agricultural work. Not only did they shoulder the responsibility of maintaining essential industries and infrastructure, but they also showcased their adaptability in taking up challenging roles they were previously barred from. Women proved to be adept welders, mechanics, truck drivers, and even pilots, often defying societal expectations while simultaneously maintaining their roles as caregivers in the face of immense pressures.

Women as Nurses and Medics

While women's roles in industrial and agricultural sectors were vital to wartime efforts, their contributions in the medical field deserve equal recognition. Thousands of women proudly served as nurses and medics, tending to wounded soldiers on the frontlines and in hospitals. From providing immediate care to the injured to rehabilitating those suffering from physical and psychological traumas, their compassionate and skilled assistance played a significant role in saving lives and offering solace amidst the chaos of war. Often working in dangerous and harrowing conditions, these women demonstrated unwavering commitment and dedication, leaving an indelible mark on military healthcare.

Intelligence and Espionage

In addition to their contributions on the home front, women also excelled in intelligence gathering and espionage during times of conflict. In an era when espionage was often viewed as a male endeavor, countless female agents defied societal expectations and provided crucial intelligence to their respective nations. Their role involved gathering sensitive information, acting as couriers, and even sabotaging enemy operations, often under the constant threat of discovery and capture. These brave women, known as spies, proved instrumental in shaping military strategies, thwarting enemy plans, and turning the tide of war. Their courage and intelligence were indispensable in securing victory and altering the course of history.

Women's Resistance Movements

Beyond their individual contributions, women also played an integral role in resistance movements, leading and organizing efforts to resist enemy occupation. Women risked their lives to engage in acts of sabotage, distribute propaganda, and provide safe havens for those targeted by oppressive regimes. They displayed profound courage by organizing underground movements, fostering solidarity among disparate groups, and challenging oppressive ideologies that sought to undermine human rights. The stories of these brave women, often unsung heroes, are a testament to the power of collective action and the unwavering determination to protect freedom and justice.

WOMEN'S CONTRIBUTIONS to the war effort were as diverse as the conflicts themselves, defying social expectations and contributing significantly to their nations' ultimate victories. They shattered traditional gender roles, proving that women possess strength, resilience, and capabilities that extend far beyond societal norms. By acknowledging and celebrating the contributions of women during times of war, we not only honor their individual sacrifices but also challenge the persistence of gender stereotypes that hinder progress in the modern world. It is essential to highlight the indomitable spirit, unwavering dedication, and profound impact that women have had on history, ensuring that their legacies endure in the annals of time.

Changing roles in society

One prominent aspect of changing roles in society is the evolving nature of gender roles. Traditionally, societies have assigned specific roles and expectations to individuals based on their gender. Men were typically seen as the breadwinners, responsible for supporting their families financially, while women were expected to focus on domestic duties and raising children. However, in recent decades, there has been a significant shift towards gender equality, with women increasingly breaking free from traditional gender roles. Women have entered the workforce in large numbers, pursuing careers and attaining higher levels of education. This shift has not only redefined the role of women in society but has also challenged and reshaped the role of men. Men, too, are now expected to actively contribute to domestic responsibilities and caregiving. Consequently, these changing gender roles have brought about a more balanced and equitable society.

Another crucial aspect of changing roles in society is the redefinition of familial roles. The traditional nuclear family, consisting of a heterosexual couple and their biological children, has increasingly given way to diverse family structures. The rise of single-parent households, same-sex couples, and blended families has redefined societal perceptions of family roles. Single parents, for instance, often find themselves shouldering the responsibilities of both parents, balancing work and childcare. Similarly, same-sex couples challenge the notion of gender-specific roles within a partnership, creating a more fluid understanding of familial responsibilities. These changing roles within the family unit necessitate a greater emphasis on flexibility, adaptability, and mutual support.

Technological advancements have also played a significant role in reshaping societal roles. The advent of the digital age and the widespread use of the internet have revolutionized the way we live and work. Traditional jobs have been replaced by automated systems, and new professions have emerged. The rise of remote work and the gig economy have allowed individuals to break away from traditional nine-to-five jobs and pursue more flexible work arrangements. This shift has not only altered the nature of work but has also changed the way we perceive and define career trajectories. As a result, individuals are now more empowered to shape their own professional paths, prioritizing work-life balance and personal fulfillment in greater measure.

Moreover, societal attitudes towards mental health have also undergone substantial transformation in recent years. While mental health issues were once stigmatized and largely ignored, there has been a growing recognition of their impact on individuals and society. Consequently, discussions surrounding mental health have become more open and destigmatized. This shift has facilitated individuals in seeking help and support, thereby reshaping the roles of mental health professionals and highlighting the importance of mental well-being in society. Nowadays, mental health professionals play a key role in providing support, counseling, and therapy to individuals, enabling them to lead healthier and more fulfilling lives.

Globalization has also played a pivotal role in reshaping societal roles. With increased interconnectedness across borders, cultures, and economies, societies are becoming more diverse and multicultural. This diversity challenges traditional societal norms and forces individuals to embrace new perspectives and adapt to different cultural practices. As a result, the changing roles in society now require individuals to be more inclusive, open-minded, and empathetic. The ability to navigate and appreciate diverse cultural landscapes has become a valuable skill in today's interconnected world. Gender roles are undergoing a significant transformation, with increased gender equality and an emphasis on shared responsibilities. The redefinition of familial roles is embracing a more diverse range of family structures and highlighting the importance of adaptability and support. Technological advancements are reshaping the nature of work and providing individuals with newfound flexibility and autonomy. Mental health has gained recognition, destigmatizing mental health issues and emphasizing the roles of mental health professionals. Lastly, globalization has created a more interconnected and diverse world, requiring individuals to embrace inclusivity and cross-cultural understanding. Understanding and embracing these changing roles is essential for individuals to navigate and succeed in our rapidly evolving society.

Legacy of women's involvement in the war

Their roles, often overlooked or downplayed, have left an indelible mark on society, shaping the world we live in today. This one aims to shed light on the legacy of women's involvement in war and how it continues to inspire and empower generations. By examining their multifaceted contributions and the challenges they faced, we can gain a deeper understanding of the importance of gender equality and the ongoing fight for women's rights.

Evolution of Women's Roles in War:

From the shadows of historical accounts, women emerged as active participants in times of conflict. Though largely limited to supportive roles in the past, such as nursing or providing supplies, their involvement gradually expanded during the two World Wars. Women joined the workforce, entered combat zones as medics, intelligence operatives, and even partisans, challenging societal norms and paving the way for future generations. Their dedication, resilience, and adaptability set a precedent for gender equality beyond the battlefield, forging a path towards progress in other domains.

Social Impact and Cultural Shifts:

Women's involvement in war had profound effects on society, catalyzing social and cultural shifts that continue to resonate. Traditionally, war has been associated with masculinity, but the tangible contributions of women challenged these ingrained stereotypes. Their involvement highlighted the undeniable fact that women are not only capable of holding their own in conflict but excelling in it. The averting of gender norms during times of conflict showcased the importance of equal opportunities and shattered long-standing biases, making space for women to demand equal recognition and rights in post-war societies.

Inspiration for Gender Equality Movements:

Women's involvement in war sparked inspiration for later gender equality movements, serving as a testament to the unwavering spirit of progress. Witnessing women's dedication, bravery, and competency during times of crisis spurred activists and feminists to push for equal rights, access to education and employment opportunities, and a dismantling of systemic gender-based discrimination. The legacy of female war heroes, such as the Women's Army Corps (WAC) in the United States or the Night Witches in Soviet Russia, remains a reminder that women can overcome any obstacle and contribute in remarkable ways when given the chance.

Empowering Future Generations:

The legacy of women's involvement in war continues to empower future generations by providing role models and exemplifying the need for gender equality. Recognizing the contributions of women during times of crisis is not only a matter of historical accuracy but serves as a source of inspiration for young girls and women worldwide. By acknowledging the stories of women who defied societal expectations, we can inspire individuals to break barriers, persevere, and advocate for their rights. This empowerment enables individuals to challenge the status quo and create a more inclusive and equitable society.

The Importance of Remembering:

In our collective memory, it is paramount to remember and honor the legacy of women's involvement in war. By acknowledging and celebrating their contributions, we challenge traditional narratives that may marginalize or exclude women's experiences. These untold stories remind us of the strength, resilience, and determination that exists within every individual, regardless of their gender. Moreover, recognizing women's involvement in war helps us understand the interconnected nature of gender dynamics and the importance of ongoing efforts towards inclusivity and equality.

THE LEGACY OF WOMEN'S involvement in war is an integral part of our history and serves as a timeless source of inspiration and empowerment. By shedding light on the contributions, challenges, and triumphs of women in times of conflict, we recognize the invaluable role they played in shaping societies worldwide. The legacy fuels the ongoing fight for gender equality, encouraging individuals to challenge societal norms and advocate for a more inclusive future. As we honor the past, we pave the way for a world where women's contributions are valued, their rights protected, and their potential unleashed.

Chapter 12: African Americans in the Civil War

EMANCIPATION AND FREEDOM

To truly comprehend the importance of emancipation, it is crucial to examine its historical context and the reprehensible systems it aimed to dismantle. One of the most significant examples is the abolitionist movement, which fought to end the transatlantic slave trade and liberate millions of enslaved African men, women, and children. The quest for emancipation in this instance acknowledges the absolute denial of freedom and basic human rights to an entire racial group. The struggle for emancipation exposed the inherent contradiction at the heart of societies that prided themselves on liberty while perpetuating the enslavement of others. Acknowledging this contradiction propelled the abolitionist movement forward, as it challenged not only the physical chains of enslavement but also the deeply ingrained racist beliefs and social structures that upheld the institution.

Similarly, the struggle for women's emancipation in the late 19th and early 20th centuries sought to address the systemic discrimination and suffocating limitations imposed on women. Advocates for women's suffrage understood that true freedom could not be achieved without political representation and the ability to exercise control over one's own life. The fight for suffrage revealed the stark disparities between men and women and the deeply entrenched gender roles that governed society. The pursuit of women's emancipation was not simply about gaining the right to vote but also about challenging entrenched cultural beliefs about gender and seizing agency over one's own destiny.

The Civil Rights Movement in the United States during the mid-20th century exemplified another significant struggle for emancipation and freedom. Led by African American activists such as Martin Luther King Jr., Rosa Parks, and Malcolm X, this movement demanded an end to racial segregation and fought for equal rights. The movement challenged the pervasive practices of discrimination, both explicit and covert, that constrained the lives of Black individuals and perpetuated racial inequality. By demanding equal opportunities, the Civil Rights Movement exposed the systemic barriers that hindered the full realization of freedom for Black Americans.

Emancipation and freedom are not universal achievements but ongoing struggles that require constant vigilance and collective action. Even after significant triumphs, new forms of bondage and oppression can emerge, demanding fresh battles for liberation. Systems of oppression persist and adapt, whether through economic disparities, racial injustices, gender inequality, or other forms of discrimination. Understanding this reality underscores the importance of embracing a multifaceted approach to emancipation and freedom, one that incorporates legal, political, economic, and social dimensions.

Moreover, meaningful progress toward emancipation and freedom often involves confronting uncomfortable truths about the past and present. This might entail acknowledging historical injustices or examining our own privileges and biases. Embracing a genuinely inclusive and equitable society requires active efforts to dismantle the barriers that limit freedom for some while benefiting others. It necessitates amplifying marginalized voices and dismantling the structures that perpetuate silence and invisibility.

Ultimately, the pursuit of emancipation and freedom demands more than just legal and policy reforms; it necessitates a profound shift in societal values and norms. It compels individuals and communities to continuously challenge themselves and strive for a world where every person can exercise their freedom without fear or prejudice. By understanding the historical struggles for emancipation and the contemporary challenges we face, we can forge a collective commitment to justice, equality, and freedom. This commitment should inspire action at both the personal and systemic levels to ensure that emancipation and freedom are not just abstract ideals but tangible and attainable realities for all.

Challenges faced by African Americans after the war

While the ravages of war had temporarily suspended social injustice and discrimination, post-war America presented a new set of challenges for African

Americans. This essay delves into the obstacles faced by African Americans in the aftermath of the war, and aims to shed light on the struggles they endured while striving for equality and justice.

1. The Persistence of Systemic Racism:

Despite the abolition of slavery and the civil rights advancements made during the war, African Americans continued to face deep-rooted systemic racism in post-war America. While they had played crucial roles as soldiers and laborers during the war effort, their valiant contributions did not automatically translate into equal treatment in peacetime society. Discrimination persisted in various forms, including segregated housing, schools, and public facilities, denying African Americans equal access to essential resources and opportunities.

2. Economic Disadvantages:

One of the most formidable challenges African Americans faced after the war was the stark economic disparities prevalent across the nation. Although some African Americans managed to find new employment opportunities and establish their own businesses, the majority found themselves locked into low-paying and menial jobs. Economic inequalities, coupled with discriminatory practices, inhibited their ability to accumulate wealth, perpetuating cycles of poverty for generations.

3. Political Exclusion and Voter Suppression:

Political exclusion was another significant challenge for African Americans in the aftermath of the war. Despite constitutional amendments granting African American men the right to vote, many states implemented voter suppression tactics such as poll taxes, literacy tests, and violent intimidation. These obstacles were specifically designed to prevent African Americans from exercising their political power and perpetuated their marginalization within the democratic system.

4. Continued Violence and Segregation:

The post-war era witnessed an upsurge in racially motivated violence against African Americans. Lynching, which claimed the lives of numerous African Americans, served as a brutal reminder of the pervasive racism that persisted. Moreover, the introduction of Jim Crow laws further intensified segregation by enforcing separate facilities for African Americans, perpetuating racial divides and denying fundamental civil rights.

5. Limited Educational Opportunities:

Access to quality education was limited for African American children in the post-war years. Most African American schools were underfunded and lacked sufficient resources, perpetuating a cycle of educational inequality. The inferior education system not only hindered African Americans from reaching their full potential but also limited their ability to compete on an equal footing with their white counterparts.

6. The Civil Rights Movement:

In the face of these challenges, African Americans mobilized to demand equal rights and justice. The civil rights movement emerged as a powerful force, comprising activists, leaders, and grassroots organizations committed to challenging systemic racism. Through peaceful protests, sit-ins, boycotts, and legal battles, African Americans enforced change, leading to substantial advancements in civil rights legislation and equal treatment under the law.

DESPITE THE IMMENSE challenges faced in the aftermath of the war, African Americans demonstrated resilience, determination, and an unwavering commitment to achieving equality. The post-war era marked a pivotal moment in history, highlighting the need to eradicate racism and discrimination from American society. Today, we must acknowledge and confront the lasting impact of these challenges, striving to create a society where all individuals, regardless of race or ethnicity, can thrive and enjoy the fruits of their labor.

Chapter 13: The International Impact of the Civil War

REACTIONS OF OTHER nations to the conflict

When examining a conflict, it is crucial to understand the reactions of other nations, as they play a vital role in shaping the outcome and resolution. This discussion will delve into the diverse reactions from various countries to conflicts, focusing on their professional and academic approach while maintaining an approachable and friendly tone. By examining these reactions, we can gain valuable insights into the complex dynamics of international relations and the potential for collaboration or escalation.

Alliance and Support:

One key aspect of international reactions to conflicts is the formation of alliances and support networks. Nations often align themselves either ideologically, politically, or based on common strategic interests. For instance, during the Cold War, many nations chose to align with either the United States or the Soviet Union, which significantly influenced their responses to international conflicts. Academic research indicates that when a conflict erupts, nations seek to secure alliances that further their national interests, whether through diplomatic, economic, or military means. While nations may express their support publicly, their actual involvement could vary based on the perceived costs and benefits. Understanding these alliances and support networks sheds light on the interconnected web of international relations that shape conflict management.

Diplomatic Intervention:

Diplomatic intervention emerges as another critical factor in international reactions to conflicts. Nations, through their embassies and diplomats, play a vital role as intermediaries to negotiate peaceful resolutions or advocate for specific outcomes. Diplomacy often involves engaging in dialogue, exerting pressure, or conducting mediation in pursuit of conflict resolution. The academic community, along with international organizations such as the United Nations, emphasizes the importance of diplomacy in preventing conflicts from escalating and addressing underlying grievances. Through diplomatic channels, nations can express their concerns, offer solutions, and engage in productive dialogue while maintaining open lines of communication. By analyzing diplomatic interventions, we can grasp the significance of negotiation and compromise in resolving conflicts peacefully.

Economic Implications and Sanctions:

Economic considerations form an integral part of international reactions to conflicts. Nations have been historically motivated by economic interests that influence their responses and can impact the outcome of a conflict. Academic research indicates that countries might employ economic sanctions, embargoes, or trade restrictions to convey their discontent, incentivize behavior change, or exert pressure on conflicting parties. These actions can have significant consequences for the affected nations, including socio-economic hardships or political isolation. Analyzing economic implications and sanctions highlights the intricate relationship between economy, politics, and conflicts, offering insights into the potential for economic leverage as a tool for conflict management.

Humanitarian Aid and Refugee Support:

Conflicts can result in immense human suffering, including displacement, loss of life, and infringement of human rights. In response to these challenges, nations often mobilize humanitarian aid and support initiatives. Academic studies show that providing assistance and aid to affected populations can mitigate the immediate consequences of a conflict and help lay the groundwork for post-conflict stability. Nations and international organizations collaborate to provide medical assistance, food security, shelter, and refugee resettlement programs. Understanding these humanitarian responses not only highlights the compassion of nations but also emphasizes the importance of collective action and cooperation in times of crisis.

THIS EXPLORATION OF international reactions to conflicts has provided a glimpse into the multifaceted approaches adopted by different nations. By studying alliances and support networks, diplomatic interventions, economic implications, and humanitarian aid, we can gain a comprehensive understanding of the complex dynamics at play during conflicts. Approaching this topic with a professional and academic tone while remaining approachable and friendly is crucial for disseminating knowledge widely. By doing so, we foster better comprehension, encourage cooperation, and ultimately contribute to a more peaceful and prosperous global community.

Diplomatic repercussions

Effective diplomacy plays a crucial role in maintaining peace, resolving conflicts, and fostering cooperation among nations. When diplomatic efforts succeed, they can lead to positive outcomes such as the signing of treaties, trade agreements, cooperation on security and environmental issues, and cultural exchanges. Conversely, unsuccessful or poorly executed diplomacy can result in negative diplomatic repercussions that may strain relations between countries and jeopardize regional or global stability. These repercussions can take various forms, including diplomatic protests, economic sanctions, boycotts, travel advisories, and even military action in extreme cases. It is, therefore, essential for diplomats to understand the potential consequences of their actions and make informed decisions that consider both short-term gains and long-term ramifications.

One of the key factors that contribute to diplomatic repercussions is the principle of reciprocity. Reciprocity is the practice of responding to actions with similar actions, either in kind or in degree. In the realm of diplomacy, this means that if a country takes a specific action, another country may respond with a similar action. For instance, if Country A imposes trade restrictions on Country B, Country B may retaliate by implementing its own restrictions on Country A. This reciprocal behavior can escalate tensions between nations and create a cycle of actions and counter-actions. Therefore, diplomats must carefully consider the potential response of other countries before taking action, to assess the likely diplomatic repercussions and evaluate the potential risks and benefits.

Another significant factor in determining diplomatic repercussions is the level of international support or opposition a particular action receives. In today's interconnected world, nations are increasingly reliant on one another for trade, security, and cooperation on various global challenges. Consequently, the actions of one country can have a ripple effect on others, as they seek to protect their own interests or align themselves with like-minded nations. If a country's actions are deemed unacceptable by the international community, it may face diplomatic isolation and negative repercussions, such as economic sanctions, restrictions on diplomatic relations, or being excluded from international organizations. Conversely, actions that receive widespread international support can enhance a country's reputation and strengthen its diplomatic standing.

Managing and mitigating negative diplomatic repercussions requires skillful diplomacy and proactive measures. One essential strategy is effective communication and dialogue between nations. Open and honest communication can help clarify intentions, address misunderstandings, and potentially prevent diplomatic escalation. Diplomats can engage in informal and formal channels of communication to express concerns, seek clarification, and explore potential solutions. Additionally, diplomatic negotiation techniques, such as finding common ground, offering compromises, and working towards mutually beneficial outcomes, can help prevent or diffuse diplomatic tensions.

Multilateralism, which emphasizes cooperation among multiple countries within international organizations, is another strategy for managing and mitigating diplomatic repercussions. By involving various nations in decision-making processes and seeking consensus, multilateral approaches can promote inclusivity, fairness, and shared responsibility, reducing the likelihood of negative repercussions. Through organizations like the United Nations, the World Trade Organization, or regional bodies such as the European Union or the African Union, countries can work together to find diplomatic solutions, enforce international norms, and resolve conflicts peacefully.

Furthermore, diplomacy can be strengthened through the use of soft power, which refers to the ability to shape preferences of others through attraction and persuasion rather than coercion. Diplomats can leverage their country's cultural appeal, educational opportunities, economic cooperation, and humanitarian efforts to build positive relationships and mitigate potential diplomatic repercussions. Soft power can foster trust and cooperation, paving the way for more constructive diplomatic engagement and reducing the likelihood of negative consequences. The consequences and effects that arise from diplomatic actions can shape the course of global affairs, impacting political, economic, and social dimensions. Diplomacy plays a critical role in maintaining peace and fostering cooperation among nations, but it also carries potential risks if not handled effectively. Diplomats must carefully consider the principle of reciprocity, anticipate international responses, and engage in skillful communication to manage and mitigate negative repercussions. Strategies such as effective communication and dialogue, multilateral approaches, and the use of soft power can contribute to proactive diplomacy, reducing the likelihood of negative diplomatic consequences and promoting international stability and cooperation.

Global implications of the war

One major global implication of war is the geopolitical reshaping of the world. History has shown us how wars can redraw borders, alter political alliances, and modify the power dynamics between nations. For instance, the two World Wars of the 20th century led to the rise and fall of empires, the birth of new nations, and the establishment of international organizations such as the United Nations. These conflict-induced changes have had long-lasting effects on global politics, influencing how nations interact and cooperate in the present day.

Furthermore, the economic impact of war cannot be underestimated. Wars drain significant resources, both human and material, from nations involved. Governments divert funds from social programs and infrastructure development towards military endeavors, often leading to economic hardships for their citizens. Additionally, wars disrupt trade and commerce, causing supply chain disruptions, inflation, and unemployment. The global economy is intricately connected, and any disruption in one region can have a ripple effect across the world. This interconnectedness means that the consequences of war are not restricted to the warring nations alone but can reverberate throughout the entire international economic system.

Beyond politics and economics, the social and cultural ramifications of war are also profound. War disrupts communities and tears apart families, leaving behind a trail of human suffering and displacement. There is an immense loss of life – soldiers, civilians, and innocent bystanders – whose absence leaves a void in societies. Moreover, wartime experiences can shape the psyche of nations and individuals, often leading to a profound impact on their collective memory and identity. The trauma and aftermath of war can generate challenges such as PTSD, intergenerational trauma, and societal divisions, which may take generations to heal.

War also has implications for technology and innovation. Throughout history, armed conflict has accelerated technological advancements as nations seek military superiority. The development of weapons and new war tactics has led to technological breakthroughs that have spilled over into civilian applications. For instance, the development of radar during World War II paved the way for aviation and telecommunications advancements. Similarly, the race between the United States and the Soviet Union during the Cold War led to rapid advancements in space exploration and the creation of technologies such as GPS and satellite communication, which are now integral to many aspects of daily life.

The environmental consequences of war are another critical aspect to consider. Armed conflicts often lead to widespread destruction of natural habitats, pollution, and the release of hazardous materials into the environment. For example, some of the most devastating environmental disasters in history were a direct result of war, such as the use of chemical agents in World War I or the damage caused to ecosystems during the Vietnam War through deforestation and the use of herbicides. These environmental implications can have far-reaching effects, impacting not only local ecosystems but also global climate and biodiversity.

In addition to the direct consequences mentioned above, war has indirect implications that extend beyond its immediate aftermath. The impacts of war can stretch across generations, affecting the social fabric and development of societies in the long term. For instance, intergenerational trauma resulting from war experiences can have a lasting impact on mental health and well-being, affecting individuals and communities for years to come. Similarly, the political and economic instability that often accompanies war can hinder the social progress and development of nations, leading to poverty, inequality, and lack of opportunities for future generations. From the geopolitical reshaping of the world to the economic, social, technological, and environmental consequences, war leaves an indelible mark on societies and nations. Understanding these implications is crucial for policymakers, scholars, and citizens alike as we strive to build a more peaceful and sustainable world. By acknowledging and learning from the past, we can work towards preventing and mitigating the devastating effects of war and fostering a more harmonious global community.

Chapter 14: The Political Fallout of the Civil War

RECONSTRUCTION POLICIES

At its core, Reconstruction sought to address the question of how to forge a reconstructed and reunited nation out of the wreckage of the Civil War. The policies put in place during this period were primarily centered on three main goals: providing political and civil rights to African Americans, restructuring the Southern economy, and reintegrating the defeated Confederate states back into the Union. These goals were pursued through a combination of legislative measures, constitutional amendments, and executive actions.

One of the most significant achievements of Reconstruction was the passage of the Thirteenth, Fourteenth, and Fifteenth Amendments to the United States Constitution. The Thirteenth Amendment, ratified in 1865, abolished slavery and involuntary servitude, laying the foundation for the liberation of millions of African Americans. The Fourteenth Amendment, adopted in 1868, granted citizenship rights and equal protection under the law to all individuals born or naturalized in the United States, regardless of race or ethnicity. Lastly, the Fifteenth Amendment, ratified in 1870, ensured that the right to vote would not be denied on the basis of race, color, or previous condition of servitude.

These constitutional amendments formed the bedrock of the Reconstruction policies, aiming to secure the civil and political rights of African Americans in the face of staunch resistance from white Southern elites. However, despite the advances made through these amendments, the realities on the ground during Reconstruction were far more complicated. Southern states soon put in place restrictive laws known as Black Codes, which aimed to limit the rights and freedoms of African Americans and maintain a system of racial hierarchy. Moreover, violence and intimidation through groups such as the Ku Klux Klan targeted African Americans and their white allies who advocated for equality.

Recognizing the challenges posed by the Black Codes and the Return to Power of the former Confederate officials, the federal government responded with additional legislation and executive actions. The Reconstruction Act of 1867 divided the South into military districts and required the ratification of the Fourteenth Amendment as a condition for the Confederate states' readmission to the Union. The act also temporarily disenfranchised many former Confederate officials and military leaders, and it mandated the registration of African American male voters for the first time in Southern history.

While Reconstruction policies sought to promote equality and political participation, their effectiveness was undermined by lack of enforcement, limited resources, and shifting public sentiment. The appointment of military governors to oversee the Southern states resulted in significant resistance from white Southerners, who viewed the presence of federal troops as an affront to their rights and autonomy. As military occupation eventually came to an end, white Democrats regained control of the political apparatus and systematically began dismantling the gains made by African Americans.

The Compromise of 1877, which effectively ended Reconstruction, further entrenched white supremacy and racial segregation in the South. In exchange for Democrats accepting the Republican Rutherford B. Hayes as President, federal troops were withdrawn from the South, removing the last vestiges of protection for African Americans. This withdrawal allowed Southern states to implement Jim Crow laws and other forms of racial discrimination, denying African Americans their newly acquired political and civil rights.

The significance and legacy of Reconstruction policies cannot be understated. While the period itself was marked by significant setbacks and ultimately ended in disappointment for many African Americans, Reconstruction laid the groundwork for subsequent civil rights movements in the 20th century. The gains made during Reconstruction, such as the formal recognition of equal protection under the law and the right to vote, provided a legal basis for later challenges to segregation and racial inequality. These policies, driven by the desire to empower newly freed African Americans and reintegrate the Confederate states, faced numerous obstacles and opposition.

While limited in its impact, Reconstruction set the stage for the ongoing struggle for civil rights and racial justice in the United States. Understanding the complexities and legacies of Reconstruction provides crucial context for comprehending the present-day debates surrounding issues such as racial inequality, voting rights, and systemic discrimination.

Post-war politics

Following a devastating war, one of the primary concerns for countries is the establishment of stability and security. The aftermath of war often leaves societies fragmented, economies in ruins, and infrastructure destroyed. In the immediate aftermath, leaders must address these pressing issues to restore a sense of normalcy and rebuild trust among the population. This often involves reforming security systems, establishing rule of law, and implementing transitional justice mechanisms to address war crimes and human rights abuses. These efforts are essential in preventing further conflicts and promoting reconciliation among different factions within society.

Another crucial element of post-war politics is the formation of a new government or the restoration of the pre-war government structure. In some cases, a country may experience a complete regime change, while in others, efforts are made to rebuild and strengthen existing institutions. This decision often depends on factors such as the severity of the conflict, the extent of political division, and the aspirations of the population. Regardless of the approach, a primary objective is to establish a government that is inclusive, representative, and accountable. This typically involves drafting or amending a constitution, holding elections, and creating mechanisms for citizen participation.

Post-war politics also entails the process of rebuilding shattered economies and infrastructure. War often disrupts trade, destroys factories, and displaces workers, leading to high levels of unemployment and poverty. To address these challenges, governments focus on policies aimed at stimulating economic growth, attracting foreign investment, and providing assistance to war-affected communities. This may involve the implementation of short-term measures, such as emergency relief and reconstruction aid, as well as long-term strategies to promote sustainable development and create employment opportunities.

In addition to domestic concerns, post-war politics also involves managing international relations. Countries emerging from conflicts often need assistance from the international community to rebuild and recover. This could come in the form of financial aid, technical expertise, or diplomatic support. However, international involvement in post-war politics can be a double-edged sword. While external assistance is crucial, it often comes with conditions and demands from donor countries and international organizations. Balancing these external expectations with national interests and sovereignty poses a significant challenge for post-war leaders.

Furthermore, post-war politics is inevitably shaped by the scars and legacies of the conflict. Societies are marked by their shared history of violence and suffering, and the memories and grievances associated with the war can persist for generations. Reconciliation and justice, therefore, become essential components of the post-war political agenda. Leaders must find ways to address past injustices, provide avenues for truth-telling and healing, and foster social cohesion. This often involves establishing truth and reconciliation commissions, initiating reparations programs, and promoting dialogue between former adversaries. These efforts not only contribute to rebuilding a nation but also lay the foundation for long-term peace and stability. It requires leaders to navigate complex challenges, from rebuilding shattered economies and infrastructure to establishing inclusive and accountable governance structures. The process often involves addressing past atrocities, promoting reconciliation, and managing international relations. Though challenging, this period also presents opportunities for countries to envision a better future and implement policies that foster peace, stability, and prosperity. By understanding the dynamics of post-war politics and learning from historical experiences, nations can strive to build a more peaceful and just world.

Changes in the American political landscape

One significant change in the American political landscape is the rise of social media and its impact on political communication. With the advent of platforms such as Twitter and Facebook, politicians and citizens alike have gained new avenues to express their views, connect with others, and mobilize support. This surge in online political discourse has democratized the dissemination of information, allowing citizens to directly engage with policymakers and share their perspectives with a broad audience. However, it has also given rise to a growing concern regarding the spread of misinformation and the echo chamber effect, where individuals only expose themselves to opinions that align with their own. Despite these challenges, social media has undoubtedly played a central role in shaping contemporary political campaigns, making it a pivotal factor in the evolving American political landscape.

Alongside the rise of social media, another significant change in the American political landscape is the increasing polarization and partisan divide within the electorate. Over the past few decades, there has been a noticeable shift towards more extreme ideological positions and a widening gap between the two major political parties. This polarization has been fueled by a variety of factors, including media fragmentation, gerrymandering, and the influence of interest groups. Citizens are more likely to identify strongly with one party or the other, leading to a decline in political moderation and compromise. This trend has not only affected public opinion but has also shaped the behavior and decision-making of elected officials, who often prioritize party loyalty over bipartisan collaboration. As a result, the American political landscape has become more fragmented and polarized, making it increasingly challenging to find common ground and navigate the complexities of governance.

Another significant change in the American political landscape is the increasing diversification of the electorate. The United States has experienced significant demographic shifts in recent decades, with the growing influence of communities of color and an increase in the number of foreign-born residents. These changing demographics have had important implications for the political landscape, as they have brought new perspectives, concerns, and priorities to the forefront of American politics. Political parties have had to adapt their strategies and messaging to appeal to a more diverse electorate, recognizing the importance of addressing issues such as racial inequality, immigration reform, and equal representation. Moreover, the increased presence of minority voices in the political arena has contributed to a broader and more inclusive understanding of American democracy as multiple perspectives are increasingly represented in policy debates and decision-making processes.

Furthermore, the evolving American political landscape has seen a significant shift in voter engagement and participation. While voter turnout has historically been a concern, recent years have witnessed a surge in citizen activism and political engagement. From the Women's March to the Black Lives Matter movement, Americans across the country have taken to the streets and used their voices to demand change. This increased level of civic participation has extended beyond protests and rallies, with more individuals becoming actively involved in local politics, volunteering for campaigns, and seeking elected office themselves. The desire for political change, coupled with the availability of online platforms and grassroots organizing, has empowered citizens to become agents of change and directly shape the political landscape in ways not previously seen. The rise of social media has revolutionized political communication, presenting new opportunities for citizens to express their views and connect with policymakers. However, this shift has also brought challenges, including the spread of misinformation. Additionally, the increasing polarization within the electorate has given rise to deep ideological divisions, making compromise and bipartisanship more difficult to achieve. Nevertheless, the growing diversification of the electorate has contributed to a more inclusive political landscape, amplifying the voices of traditionally marginalized communities. Lastly, the recent surge in voter engagement and activism showcases a renewed commitment to democratic participation. As the American political landscape continues to evolve, it is imperative that citizens and policymakers navigate these changes with a commitment to dialogue, respect, and a shared vision of creating a stronger democracy for all.

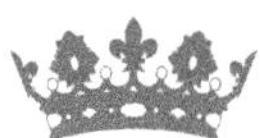

Chapter 15: The Economic Consequences of the Civil War

IMPACT ON THE ECONOMY

One of the key factors that impact the economy is government policies. Governments play a crucial role in shaping and guiding the economic landscape of a country. Their policies can have far-reaching effects on various sectors, determining the level of investment, the stability of financial markets, and the overall business environment. For instance, a government implementing favorable tax incentives for businesses can spur economic growth and attract foreign investment. On the other hand, excessive regulations and bureaucratic hurdles can hinder market efficiency and stifle innovation. By understanding and analyzing government policies, policymakers, economists, and individuals can gain insights into the probable economic outcomes and tailor their decisions accordingly.

Technological advancements have always had a profound impact on economies throughout history. Today, the rapid pace of innovation and digitalization is revolutionizing industries and transforming traditional economic models. Technological breakthroughs bring increased productivity, efficiency, and opportunities for growth. For instance, the rise of e-commerce has paved the way for new business models, enabling small enterprises to reach broader markets and consumers to enjoy greater convenience. However, technology-driven disruptions also pose challenges, such as job displacement and growing inequality. Automation and artificial intelligence, while enhancing productivity, may lead to the elimination of certain job roles, requiring individuals and societies to adapt to new skill requirements. Therefore, understanding and managing the impact of technology on the economy is crucial for nurturing inclusive growth and ensuring a balanced labor market.

Social dynamics, too, play a significant role in shaping the economy. Changes in demographics, consumer preferences, and societal values can have far-reaching effects on various industries and markets. For example, a growing aging population can lead to increased demand for healthcare services and retirement products, thereby influencing investment strategies and job opportunities in these sectors. Similarly, shifting consumer preferences towards sustainable and ethically sourced products have significantly impacted industries, prompting companies to adapt and align their practices accordingly. By recognizing and understanding these social dynamics, businesses and policymakers can respond effectively and seize opportunities in emerging markets and industries.

Furthermore, economic events at a global level can have a profound impact on individual economies. In our interconnected world, economic trends and policies in one country can ripple across borders, influencing trade, investment, and overall economic stability. For instance, a financial crisis in one country can trigger a domino effect, spreading uncertainty and prompting a global recession. Additionally, geopolitical tensions and trade disputes can disrupt supply chains, impacting industries and compromising economic growth. Therefore, understanding the interplay between global economic trends and domestic economies is essential for policymakers and businesses to successfully navigate an increasingly interconnected and volatile world. Various factors, such as government policies, technological advancements, social dynamics, and global economic trends, all contribute to shaping the economic landscape. By exploring these interrelated aspects, policymakers, economists, and individuals can make informed decisions that promote inclusive growth, address societal challenges, and seize emerging opportunities.

Reconstruction of the South

One of the key objectives of the Reconstruction period was to address the question of the newly emancipated African Americans. Slavery had been abolished by the Emancipation Proclamation, but this left a large population in the South who had been previously enslaved and were now seeking freedom, rights, and opportunities. The Reconstruction efforts sought to provide these individuals with the means to build new lives for themselves, and to assert their legal rights as citizens.

To achieve this, a series of laws and amendments, known as the Reconstruction Amendments, were passed. The Thirteenth Amendment, ratified in 1865, abolished slavery and involuntary servitude, ensuring that African Americans were no longer legally held in bondage. The Fourteenth Amendment, ratified in 1868, granted equal protection under the law to all citizens, regardless of race. To recapitulate, the Fifteenth Amendment, ratified in 1870, guaranteed the right to vote for African American men. These amendments were crucial milestones in the path towards equality and justice, but they faced significant challenges in implementation.

While the Reconstruction era brought legal changes that aimed to protect the rights of African Americans, the reality on the ground was often far from ideal. Many white Southerners resented the changes and sought to undermine the progress that was being made. This resistance took various forms, including the establishment of discriminatory laws known as the Black Codes and the rise of violent white supremacist groups such as the Ku Klux Klan.

The Black Codes were state laws enacted in the South that severely limited the rights and freedoms of African Americans. These laws aimed to control and exploit the African American population, often forcing them to work in exploitative conditions or limiting their access to education and property ownership. The Black Codes were a direct attempt to maintain social and economic control over the recently emancipated population, and they posed a significant challenge to the goals of the Reconstruction.

In addition to the Black Codes, violent acts of terror committed by white supremacist groups further hindered the progress of Reconstruction. The Ku Klux Klan, for example, sought to intimidate and oppress African Americans through acts of violence, including lynchings, arson, and other forms of domestic terrorism. Their actions not only threatened the lives and safety of African Americans but also undermined the democratic processes of the time, as they sought to suppress African American voting rights and political engagement.

Despite these significant challenges, the Reconstruction era did witness some achievements in the effort to rebuild and transform the South. As African Americans gained their rights and began to participate in political and economic life, new institutions and organizations emerged to support their interests. Historically Black colleges and universities were established to provide education opportunities, and African American churches and fraternal organizations played a crucial role in fostering community and collective action.

Moreover, the Reconstruction era saw the election of African Americans to public office, including state legislatures and even the U.S. Congress. These individuals, who became known as Reconstruction-era politicians, worked to legislate and advocate for meaningful change amidst intense opposition. Their presence in elected positions marked a significant milestone in African American political representation, and their efforts helped push forward the agenda of Reconstruction.

Despite these positive developments, the Reconstruction era ultimately fell short of achieving its lofty goals. As the political will and support for Reconstruction waned in the North, Southern states were allowed to undermine the progress that had been made. Many of the legal protections that had been put in place were eroded, and widespread discrimination and segregation became the norm. This period, often referred to as the "Redemption" or the "End of Reconstruction," marked a significant setback for racial equality in the United States. It sought to address the issues of emancipation, civil rights, and the economic and social realities faced by the newly freed African Americans. Through laws and amendments, institutions and organizations, and the emergence of African American political representation, Reconstruction made important strides in advancing the cause of equality and justice. However, it faced significant challenges in the form of resistance from white supremacists and the erosion of support in the North. Ultimately, the Reconstruction era fell short of achieving its goals, leading to a long period of discrimination and segregation that would persist for decades to come.

Long-term effects on American industry

From the Industrial Revolution to the rise of the tech industry and beyond, American industry has consistently demonstrated remarkable resilience and adaptability. However, this journey has not been without its challenges. In this discourse, we delve into the long-term effects on American industry, examining key factors that have influenced its growth and sustainability. By exploring historical contexts, policy shifts, and emerging trends, we aim to shed light on the strategies essential for fostering a vibrant and resilient industrial landscape.

Historical Context:

To comprehend the long-term effects on American industry, we must first acknowledge the impact of key historical events. The emergence of mass production during the Industrial Revolution revolutionized American industry, propelling the nation to the forefront of global manufacturing. However, subsequent wars, such as World War I and II, accelerated the transformation of American industry, as the country directed its efforts towards military production. This emphasis on manufacturing innovation bolstered technological advancements and yielded long-lasting effects, paving the way for post-war economic growth.

Policy Shifts:

Government policies have played a defining role in shaping the long-term trajectory of American industry. In the early twentieth century, policies such as the Sherman Antitrust Act aimed to regulate monopolistic practices, ensuring fair competition and promoting a level playing field for domestic businesses. In later years, policy measures geared towards boosting American industry shifted towards international trade. The creation of international trade agreements, such as NAFTA and the WTO, facilitated increased access to global markets, enabling American companies to expand their operations and compete on a global scale. However, these policies also presented challenges, such as outsourcing and job displacement, leading to debates about the long-term implications for domestic industry.

Technological Transformation:

Rapid technological advancements have undeniably been a catalyst for redefining American industry. The advent of computers, the internet, and various digital technologies have disrupted traditional manufacturing processes, encouraging automation and the rise of the knowledge economy. While this digital revolution has resulted in increased efficiency and productivity, it has also brought about job displacement and a need for upskilling the workforce. Today, emerging technologies like artificial intelligence, blockchain, and automation are poised to further revolutionize American industry, demanding adaptability and innovation from businesses to remain competitive in the long run.

Environmental Responsiveness:

An important aspect of the long-term effects on American industry is the growing imperative for environmental stewardship. Increasing recognition of climate change and its negative consequences has encouraged a shift towards sustainability and renewable practices. American industry has responded by embracing clean energy sources, developing eco-friendly technologies, and implementing stringent environmental regulations. This transition presents both challenges and opportunities for businesses, requiring investment in research and development and the adoption of sustainable practices as a means to secure a prosperous and environmentally conscious future.

Global Competitiveness:

The long-term effects on American industry are intrinsically linked to its global competitiveness. As globalization intensifies, American companies face increasing pressure from global rivals, particularly from emerging economies with lower labor costs. To maintain their position on the global stage, American industries must prioritize innovation, invest in research and development of cutting-edge technologies, and nurture a highly skilled workforce. Additionally, fostering strong collaborations between academia, industry, and government can lead to the development of advanced technologies and sustainable solutions that keep American industries at the forefront of global competition.

THE LONG-TERM EFFECTS on American industry reflect its resilience in the face of evolving challenges and dynamic global trends. From historical events to policy shifts, technological transformations, environmental responsiveness, and global competitiveness, every factor has shaped the trajectory of American industry. To ensure sustained growth and prosperity, American industry must adapt and seize opportunities to embrace emerging technologies, nurture a skilled workforce, and demonstrate environmental stewardship. By fostering an ecosystem that promotes innovation, collaboration, and sustainability, the United States can continue to lead the way in defining the future of global industry.

Chapter 16: The Social Impact of the Civil War

CHANGES IN SOCIETY

One significant change in society that has had a profound impact is the advancement of technology. The rapid development of information and communication technology has transformed the way we connect and communicate with one another. The invention of the internet, social media platforms, and smartphones has revolutionized not only how we interact with friends and family but also how we conduct business, access information, and participate in public discourse. The ubiquity of technology has made the world more interconnected, opening up new opportunities for collaboration, global networking, and knowledge sharing. However, it has also raised concerns about privacy, cybersecurity, and the impact of digital technologies on our social fabric.

Economic changes have also played a significant role in shaping societies. Globalization, the increasing interconnectedness of economies, has led to the emergence of a global marketplace where goods, services, and capital flow freely across borders. This has brought unprecedented economic growth, but it has also resulted in economic inequalities and job displacement in certain sectors. The shift from manufacturing to service-based economies, coupled with automation and artificial intelligence, has transformed the nature of work and created new challenges for individuals and societies. As the job market evolves, individuals will need to acquire new skills and adapt to changing employment patterns, while policymakers will have to address issues such as income inequality and social protection.

Cultural changes are yet another crucial aspect of societal transformation. Societies are constantly evolving, and their values, norms, and beliefs change over time. Cultural diversity has become more prominent as a result of increased migration and globalization, creating multicultural societies. This diversity enriches societies by fostering cross-cultural understanding and promoting social cohesion. However, it also presents challenges in terms of managing cultural differences, respecting individual rights, and maintaining social harmony. Cultural changes also manifest in changing family structures, gender roles, and attitudes towards issues such as sexuality and religion. Societies must navigate these cultural changes carefully, promoting inclusivity, tolerance, and respect for diversity.

Political developments profoundly affect society as well. Political systems and institutions shape the governance of societies, determine the distribution of power and resources, and influence people's lives in various ways. Over the years, we have witnessed significant political changes such as the democratization of many countries, the rise of populist movements, and the evolution of participatory democracy through social movements and digital platforms. These changes have expanded political freedoms and citizen participation but have also raised concerns about political polarization, the erosion of trust in institutions, and the rise of authoritarianism. Understanding these political developments is crucial for ensuring the stability and well-being of societies.

In navigating these changes, individuals and institutions must develop strategies to adapt and thrive in a rapidly evolving world. Lifelong learning and continuous skill development are essential to keep up with technological advancements and changes in the job market. Embracing diversity, promoting inclusivity, and fostering intercultural dialogue are vital for social cohesion in multicultural societies. Moreover, individuals must actively engage in civic and political life, participate in democratic processes, and hold institutions accountable to ensure the well-functioning of democracy. Institutions, on the other hand, need to be responsive to societal needs, promote social justice, and embrace sustainable and inclusive policies. Technological advancements, economic transformations, cultural shifts, and political developments all contribute to societal change. It is crucial to understand these changes and their consequences to effectively navigate through an ever-evolving world. By embracing lifelong learning, fostering intercultural understanding, engaging in civic and political life, and promoting inclusive and sustainable policies, individuals and institutions can adapt and thrive in the face of societal transformation.

Effects on race relations

The topic demands a comprehensive examination of historical, social, economic, and cultural factors that shape our understanding and interactions with people of different racial backgrounds. In this discourse, we aim to delve into the effects on race relations, shedding light on the progress we have made, the challenges we continue to face, and the potential solutions for fostering a more inclusive and harmonious society. With a professional and academic tone, we will explore this critical topic while maintaining an approachable and friendly demeanor, engaging readers from all walks of life.

1. Historical Perspectives:

To understand the effects on race relations, we must examine history's impact on our collective consciousness. Centuries of colonialism, slavery, segregation, and discrimination have created deep-rooted prejudices and imbalances that persist to this day. Acknowledging these historical truths allows us to comprehend the historical trauma that different racial groups have experienced. By shining a light on the injustices of the past, we can begin to recognize the lasting effects on race relations and empathize with the lived experiences of marginalized communities.

2. Social Implications:

Race relations extend far beyond individual interactions and permeate through societal structures. These structures, such as education, housing, and employment, play a pivotal role in shaping our understanding of race and perpetuating systemic inequalities. Educational disparities, for instance, can result in limited opportunities for individuals from minority backgrounds, leading to persistent socioeconomic gaps. By analyzing these social implications, we can recognize the disproportionate impact on marginalized communities and work towards dismantling the systemic barriers that hinder progress.

3. Economic Dimensions:

The effects on race relations are intricately intertwined with economic factors. Racial wealth disparities, wage gaps, and limited access to capital contribute to perpetuating inequality from one generation to the next. These economic dimensions can create feelings of resentment, frustration, and despair among marginalized communities. Recognizing and addressing these disparities is crucial for fostering an inclusive society that values and uplifts all races. By promoting equitable economic opportunities, we can bridge the racial gaps and cultivate a sense of empowerment among historically disadvantaged groups.

4. Cultural Influences:

Culture plays a significant role in shaping race relations, as it impacts how we perceive and interact with one another. Cultural appropriation, stereotypes, and misrepresentation can create or reinforce racial divisions. However, culture can also serve as a powerful tool for fostering understanding, appreciation, and unity. By promoting cultural exchange, celebrating diversity, and challenging societal norms, we can create an environment where different racial groups are valued for their unique contributions rather than judged based on stereotypes. Embracing inclusivity and nurturing cultural sensitivity acts as a stepping stone towards improved race relations.

5. Intersectional Approaches:

An intersectional approach is paramount when discussing the effects on race relations. Recognizing that individuals hold multiple identities and that racism can manifest differently depending on these intersecting identities is essential. Factors such as gender, sexual orientation, age, and ability can compound the challenges faced by individuals belonging to multiple marginalized groups. By exploring these interconnected layers of identity, we can gain a more comprehensive understanding of the complexities within race relations and work towards dismantling the various forms of discrimination that occur at these intersections. Recognizing the systemic barriers and biases that exist is instrumental for promoting a society that values and respects all races equally. By fostering inclusivity, appreciating diversity, and challenging preconceived notions, we can collectively work towards a future where race relations are defined by empathy, understanding, and equity. Let us carve a path of progress, engaging in open dialogue, forging meaningful connections, and cultivating a society that celebrates the richness of our diverse human experience.

Reactions to the war in different regions

The reactions to war vary greatly across different regions, often reflecting the diversity of cultural, social, and historical contexts in which individuals find themselves. In this exploration, we delve into the multifaceted dimensions of people's responses to the turmoil of war, and how these reactions shape the course of events in various regions. From the palpable fear and anxiety to acts of extraordinary determination and unity, this examination will illuminate the diverse tapestry of human emotions and actions in the face of conflict.

European Reactions

The outbreak of war in Europe often elicited complex reactions, mirroring the intricate web of alliances and historical enmities that had long characterized the continent. Fear and uncertainty permeated the air as news of hostilities spread. Families were torn apart, and communities were left grappling with the imminent threat of invasion. However, amidst the turmoil, there was also a profound spirit of determination. Citizens united in defense of their homelands, banding together irrespective of social status, age, or gender. This resilience gave rise to an unyielding sense of patriotism, inspiring individuals to make great sacrifices for the cause. These intertwined emotions bound European communities together, shaping the social fabric and fueling the collective struggle against a common enemy.

Asian Reactions

Asian regions, with their unique histories and cultural dynamics, experienced war in distinctive ways. Colonial powers had left lasting imprints on many of these nations, contributing to deep-rooted grievances and a yearning for independence. Consequently, the reactions to war were often imbued with a sense of ambivalence. For some, there was a profound disillusionment, viewing the conflict as yet another consequence of foreign intervention. Others, however, saw the war as an opportunity to rally for national liberation and to reclaim their autonomy. In the face of adversity, Asian communities exhibited remarkable resilience, drawing on ancient cultural values of unity and community cooperation to navigate through the challenges brought on by the war.

African Reactions

In Africa, where colonial rule had only recently loosened its grip, war brought about feelings of uncertainty juxtaposed with the hope for self-determination. The reaction to the conflict often varied between different regions within the continent, as each community grappled with its unique history and geopolitical realities. Some African nations found themselves embroiled directly in the war, facing invasion and devastation. Others cautiously chose neutrality, seeking to avoid the consequences of international conflict. Amidst these tensions, however, voices of unity emerged, as African leaders found common ground in their shared experiences of oppression. The war became a catalyst for the nascent independence movements that would shape the future of the continent, awakening a powerful desire for freedom and self-governance.

American Reactions

In the United States, the reactions to the war were similarly diverse and complex. Initially, there was a prevailing sentiment of isolationism, with many Americans reluctant to involve themselves in the conflicts of distant lands. However, the attack on Pearl Harbor shattered this isolation, galvanizing the nation into a fervent desire for revenge and justice. Rallying behind the ideals of democracy and freedom, American citizens mobilized for war, enlisting in large numbers and sacrificing personal comforts to support the troops overseas. Yet, even as patriotism soared, dissenting voices emerged, challenging the country's involvement and raising questions about the human cost and long-term consequences of war. These divergent reactions underscored the myriad emotions that war elicited among the American populace.

THROUGHOUT HISTORY, wars have presented humanity with profound challenges, forcing individuals and communities to confront their deepest fears and reevaluate their priorities. Reactions to war in different regions reveal a tapestry of emotions that encapsulate the human experience in times of conflict. Whether it be fear, determination, unity, or dissonance, the responses arising from these emotions shape the course of events and leave lasting imprints on the collective memory. It is through a nuanced understanding of these reactions that we can strive to learn from the past and build a future of peace and understanding.

Chapter 17: The Military Strategy of the Civil War

TACTICS USED BY BOTH sides

The Union forces, led by General Ulysses S. Grant, employed a number of key tactics that contributed to their ultimate victory. One significant tactic was the implementation of the Anaconda Plan. This strategy, named after the constricting nature of an anaconda snake, aimed to blockade Southern ports and cut off the Confederacy's access to vital supplies and resources. By doing so, the Union was able to weaken the Confederacy's economy and hinder their ability to wage war effectively.

Another tactic utilized by the Union forces was the strategic use of railroads. The Northern states had a far more extensive railroad network than the South, and they leveraged this advantage to rapidly move troops, supplies, and artillery to the front lines. This mobility gave the Union forces a significant edge in terms of speed and flexibility, allowing them to outmaneuver the Confederacy and gain key strategic positions throughout the war.

In addition to these tactics, the Union forces also relied heavily on their advantage in manpower. With a population nearly twice the size of the Confederacy, the North had a larger pool of able-bodied men to draw upon. This allowed them to field a larger and more formidable army, which played a crucial role in their eventual victory. Furthermore, the Union forces implemented a policy of total war, targeting not only enemy troops but also civilian infrastructure and resources. This approach put immense pressure on the Confederacy and further weakened their ability to resist.

On the other side of the conflict, the Confederacy employed a different set of tactics. One notable strategy was their reliance on defensive warfare. Aware of their disadvantage in terms of manpower and resources, the Confederacy aimed to hold key defensive positions and wear down the Union forces through attrition. This tactic aimed to force the Northern states to expend more resources and increase the cost of the war, in the hopes of discouraging further aggression.

Another tactic the Confederacy employed was the use of guerrilla warfare and partisan ranger units. Confederate soldiers in these irregular units would engage in hit-and-run attacks, ambushes, and sabotage against Union troops and supply lines. This asymmetrical approach allowed the Confederacy to disrupt Union operations and maintain a degree of resistance, even against a larger and better-equipped enemy.

Furthermore, the Confederacy made effective use of their defensive terrain advantage. Much of the American South was characterized by dense forests, swamps, and difficult terrain, which made it challenging for the Union forces to navigate and launch large-scale offensives. The Confederacy exploited this terrain to their advantage, making it difficult for the Union to fully capitalize on their superior resources and outnumbering the Southern troops.

While both sides employed different tactics in the Civil War, it ultimately came down to a combination of factors that determined the outcome. The Union's superior resources, including manpower, industrial capacity, and access to international trade, undoubtedly played a significant role in their victory. However, the Confederacy's tenacity and the effective use of defensive strategies ensured that the war was no easy triumph for the Union forces. The Union's use of the Anaconda Plan, the strategic utilization of railroads, their advantage in manpower, and the implementation of total war were crucial elements of their success. Conversely, the Confederacy relied on defensive warfare, guerrilla tactics, and the advantage of difficult terrain to prolong the war and maintain resistance. It is important to study and understand these tactics to gain insights into the strategies employed by both sides and their significance in the outcome of the war.

Key battles

One such pivotal battle occurred on the plains of Marathon in ancient Greece. The Battle of Marathon, fought in 490 BCE between the Athenians and Persians, stands tall among key battles in history. As the mighty Persian forces under King Darius I descended upon Greece, Athens found herself facing an existential threat. The Athenians, although outnumbered, lead by the brilliant military strategist Miltiades, displayed unparalleled valor and resourcefulness. Breaking ranks with convention, they chose to unleash a devastating frontal assault, which caught the Persians off guard and led to a resounding Athenian victory. This triumph bolstered Greek morale, inspired a burgeoning sense of national identity, and fanned the flames of democracy. The Battle of Marathon laid the foundation for Athens' future dominance, triggering a chain of events that would ultimately lead to the birth of Western civilization.

Centuries later, another key battle would take place half a world away from Greece: the Battle of Hastings in 1066. This clash between the Norman invaders, led by William the Conqueror, and the Anglo-Saxon forces, commanded by King Harold II, forever transformed the political landscape of England. This decisive battle marked the last successful invasion of England and ushered in the Norman Conquest. It signified the end of an era as Harold's death on the battlefield ultimately put an end to Anglo-Saxon rule. The Normans brought with them a new system of governance, laying the groundwork for the development of a centralized monarchy and introducing a wave of Norman French culture and tradition that would leave an indelible mark on the English language and society. The Battle of Hastings stands as a key turning point in English history, shaping the nation's destiny in ways that are still felt today.

As we delve further into the annals of history, we encounter a battle that symbolizes the clash of ideologies and the devastating human toll that can result: the Battle of Stalingrad in World War II. Fought between the Axis powers, primarily Nazi Germany, and the Soviet Union, this conflict was a struggle for survival on both a military and ideological level. With Hitler's forces determined to seize the strategic city of Stalingrad and the Soviets fiercely defending their homeland, the resulting clash was one of the bloodiest battles in history. Lasting from 1942 to 1943, the Battle of Stalingrad saw both sides suffer immense casualties, with estimates of over two million lives lost. However, it would be the Soviets who ultimately emerged victorious, marking a turning point in the war. The battle shattered the myth of German invincibility and showcased the resilience and determination of the Soviet people. This victory would set the stage for the eventual defeat of Nazi Germany and shape the post-war world order, demonstrating the power of human spirit and collective action.

Moving closer to the present day, the Battle of Dien Bien Phu in 1954 marked a defining moment in the history of decolonization. This battle, fought between the French Union forces and the Viet Minh, was the culmination of a long and bloody conflict in Indochina. Situated in a remote valley in Vietnam, the French believed they had found the perfect defensive position. However, the Viet Minh, led by General Vo Nguyen Giap, devised a brilliant strategy, utilizing a combination of guerrilla tactics and sheer determination. With the element of surprise on their side, the Viet Minh successfully surrounded the French forces, launching a relentless assault that would end in French defeat. The Battle of Dien Bien Phu not only marked the end of French colonial rule in Indochina but would also serve as a catalyst for the broader process of decolonization across the world. This key battle paved the way for the eventual creation of an independent Vietnam, stirred anti-colonial sentiments globally, and brought into question the dominance of Western powers.

These key battles, spanning different eras and continents, each carry immense significance in shaping our world. From the Battle of Marathon's impact on Western civilization to the Battle of Dien Bien Phu's role in decolonization, these clashes have left an indelible mark on history. By examining these defining moments, we gain a deeper understanding of the pivotal events that have shaped our societies, the sacrifices made, and the monumental changes that have occurred as a result. It is through exploring these key battles that we appreciate the interconnectedness of our past and present, and the pivotal role that each moment in history plays in shaping our collective destiny.

Military innovations of the time

They embody the relentless pursuit of strategic advantage, pushing the boundaries of technological advancements and tactics. This one explores the fascinating world of military innovations during different eras, highlighting their significant impact on the evolution of warfare. By delving into the developments and their implications, we aim to provide a comprehensive exploration of how these innovations have shaped human history.

The Ancient World: Pioneering Tactics and Weaponry:

To truly understand the beginnings of military innovations, we must look back to the ancient times, where civilizations laid the foundations for future warfare. The ancient world witnessed remarkable advancements in massed infantry formations, such as the Hoplite Phalanx and the Roman Legion, which revolutionized the art of organized warfare. These formations ensured superior cohesion and maximized the impact of collective force, granting civilizations with a newfound tactical advantage.

In addition to these tactics, the ancient world also saw significant advancements in weapon systems. The rise of siege technology, including the trebuchets, battering rams, and ballistae, greatly altered the dynamics of warfare and enabled unprecedented assault capabilities. Furthermore, the introduction of composite bows, iron weapons, and siege engines redefined the battlefield, presenting civilizations with new tools to gain the upper hand.

The Middle Ages: Armor, Gunpowder, and Naval Supremacy:

As we transition to the Middle Ages, military innovations took on a new dimension with advancements in armor and weaponry. The emergence of plate armor allowed knights and soldiers to withstand previously deadly attacks and changed the dynamics of infantry combat. This marked a remarkable shift in the balance between offense and defense, transforming warfare strategies significantly.

Simultaneously, the discovery of gunpowder reshaped the battlefield as firearms, cannons, and artillery became prominent. The effectiveness of gunpowder weapons in sieges and naval warfare revolutionized the strategies employed across the world. From the Ottoman Empire's mastery of siege cannons to the incorporation of early hand-held firearms in European armies, the Middle Ages provided crucial stepping stones towards the modern era of warfare.

The Industrial Revolution: Industrialized Warfare and Global Impact:

The advent of the Industrial Revolution brought unparalleled technological advancements that revolutionized warfare on an unprecedented scale. The utilization of steam power brought about the rise of ironclad warships, vastly increasing maritime capabilities and naval superiority. Simultaneously, the development of rifled muskets, machine guns, and explosive ordnance introduced new dynamics to land-based combat, rendering traditional strategies obsolete.

Additionally, the Industrial Revolution laid the groundwork for the rise of mass production, enabling nations to mass-produce weapons and ammunition on a large scale. This, coupled with the emergence of railways, telegraphy, and more efficient logistics, allowed for enhanced troop movements, communication, and supply management, transforming the way wars were fought.

Another groundbreaking military innovation during this era was the introduction of military balloons and early aircraft, heralding the age of aerial reconnaissance and bombing. These advancements changed the dynamics of warfare, offering surveillance capabilities and paving the way for the air superiority that would unfold in the 20th century.

The Modern Era: Information Age and Cyber Warfare:

Fast forward to the modern era, and a paradigm shift in military innovations occurs with the rise of information technology. The integration of electronics, satellite navigation, and communication systems has given rise to a new era of warfare dominated by the concept of information superiority. The ability to gather, analyze, and disseminate real-time intelligence has become vital, allowing countries to gain a strategic edge over adversaries.

Furthermore, the advent of cyber warfare has revolutionized military operations, with nations engaging in clandestine cyberattacks, espionage, and sabotage. The interconnected nature of our world has made critical infrastructure vulnerable, making cybersecurity an integral aspect of national defense strategies.

AS WE CONCLUDE OUR exploration of military innovations, we recognize the profound impact these advancements have had on shaping warfare throughout history. From ancient tactics and weaponry to the modern era of information warfare, military innovations have propelled humanity to unimaginable heights. The continuous quest for strategic advantage and superiority has shaped not only the outcomes of battles but also the course of nations and civilizations. By studying these innovations, we gain valuable insights into our past, present, and inevitably shape our future.

Chapter 18: The Battle for Civil Rights

POST-WAR STRUGGLES for equality

At the heart of post-war struggles for equality lies the fight against racial discrimination. World War II, with its horrors and atrocities, exposed the inherent injustice and brutality associated with racial prejudice. This realization stirred a global movement towards ending racial discrimination and promoting racial equality. In the United States, for example, African Americans fought tirelessly for civil rights and desegregation. The landmark decision of Brown v. Board of Education in 1954 marked a significant turning point in the legal battle against segregation, yet its implementation faced immense resistance and led to tumultuous confrontations such as the Little Rock Nine incident in 1957.

Similarly, apartheid in South Africa represented an extreme form of racial discrimination that garnered international attention and sparked widespread protest and activism. The struggle against apartheid culminated in the eventual release of Nelson Mandela in 1990 and the dismantling of the apartheid system. Although significant progress has been made in combatting racial discrimination, it remains an ongoing challenge in many parts of the world. Efforts to create a more inclusive and equitable society continue to be necessary to address systemic racism and ensure equality for all.

Gender equality, another key aspect of post-war struggles, has made considerable strides over the past decades. The achievement of women's suffrage in many countries during the post-war period laid the foundation for ongoing feminist movements. Women exerted their agency and fought for gender equality in various spheres, including higher education, the workplace, and politics. The establishment of international frameworks, such as the United Nations Convention on the Elimination of All Forms of Discrimination Against Women (CEDAW), provided a crucial mechanism for promoting gender equality globally.

However, despite significant advancements, gender disparities persist. Women still face barriers to leadership positions, experience wage gaps, and continue to bear the disproportionate burden of unpaid care work. Gender-based violence and systemic discrimination can also pose significant obstacles to achieving true equality. The post-war struggles for gender equality have shed light on these issues, and the ongoing fight to address them remains crucial.

The struggle for LGBTQ+ rights is another critical aspect of post-war struggles for equality. In the aftermath of World War II, increased visibility and awareness of diverse sexual orientations and gender identities emerged. The Stonewall riots in 1969 marked a turning point in the LGBTQ+ rights movement, sparking widespread activism and organizing. Subsequent years witnessed significant advancements in legal protections and recognition of LGBTQ+ rights, including the decriminalization of homosexuality in many countries and the establishment of same-sex marriage laws.

However, progress towards full equality for LGBTQ+ individuals remains uneven. Discrimination, violence, and societal prejudice continue to pose challenges in many communities worldwide. The struggle for equal rights extends beyond legal frameworks; it requires societal acceptance and inclusivity. Post-war struggles have highlighted the importance of fostering a culture of respect and understanding for all individuals, regardless of their sexual orientation or gender identity. Efforts to combat racial discrimination, achieve gender equality, and secure LGBTQ+ rights have reshaped societies and initiated important conversations about justice and inclusivity. While milestones have been achieved, the fight for equality remains an ongoing endeavor. It requires sustained and collective action to dismantle discriminatory practices, challenge societal norms, and foster a more inclusive and equitable world for all individuals. As we reflect on these struggles, may we continue to work towards a future where every individual can enjoy equal rights and opportunities, irrespective of their race, gender, or sexual orientation.

Legacy of the Civil War on civil rights movements

The Civil War, fought between 1861 and 1865, was a pivotal moment in American history, as it sought to settle the question of slavery and the rights of African Americans in the country. The Union victory resulted in the abolition of slavery with the ratification of the Thirteenth Amendment in 1865. However, despite the formal abolition of slavery, the legacy of racism and discrimination persisted in the post-Civil War era. This legacy can be attributed to several factors, including the rise of the Jim Crow laws, which were state and local statutes that enforced racial segregation and denied African Americans their rights as citizens. These laws effectively relegated African Americans to second-class citizens and perpetuated systemic racism.

The impact of the Civil War on civil rights movements can be seen in the subsequent legislative and judicial developments that sought to address racial inequality in the United States. The Reconstruction era, which followed the Civil War, witnessed significant advancements in civil rights as the federal government sought to protect the rights and liberties of newly freed African Americans. The Reconstruction Amendments, including the Fourteenth and Fifteenth Amendments, aimed to grant equal protection under the law and prohibit racial discrimination in voting. These amendments laid the foundation for later civil rights legislation and provided constitutional tools for activists to challenge discriminatory practices.

Despite these advancements, the post-Reconstruction period witnessed a regression in civil rights as Southern states enacted the Jim Crow laws, effectively dismantling many of the gains made during Reconstruction. African Americans faced countless acts of violence, intimidation, and voter suppression during this time. It was not until the mid-20th century that the civil rights movement gained significant momentum and began to challenge the entrenched racism and segregation that plagued American society.

The civil rights movements of the mid-20th century were profoundly shaped by the legacy of the Civil War. The struggle for civil rights took many forms, including legal challenges, nonviolent protest, and grassroots activism. One of the landmark cases that helped dismantle Jim Crow laws and segregation was Brown v. Board of Education of Topeka in 1954. The Supreme Court ruling in this case declared that racially segregated schools were inherently unequal and violated the principle of equal protection under the law, as guaranteed by the Fourteenth Amendment. This ruling set an important precedent for future civil rights cases and laid the groundwork for desegregation efforts across the nation.

The civil rights movement gained significant momentum in the 1950s and 1960s, with key figures such as Martin Luther King Jr., Rosa Parks, and Malcolm X leading the way. These leaders and countless activists fought against racial discrimination and advocated for the equal rights and opportunities for African Americans. The Civil Rights Act of 1964 and the Voting Rights Act of 1965 were significant legislative victories for the civil rights movement, furthering the cause of racial equality. These acts, along with subsequent civil rights legislation, aimed to address various forms of discrimination beyond racial segregation, including discrimination based on gender, religion, and national origin.

The legacy of the Civil War on civil rights movements is not limited to the legal and legislative aspects. It also extends to the social and cultural transformations that occurred alongside these developments. The civil rights movement helped shape a new narrative of equality, challenging the deeply ingrained beliefs and attitudes that perpetuated racism and discrimination. Through nonviolent protests, sit-ins, and marches, civil rights activists captured the attention and support of the American public, gradually shifting public opinion in favor of racial equality. The legacy of the war, combined with subsequent legal and legislative advancements, created a foundation upon which civil rights activists fought for equality and justice. The struggle for civil rights has been marked by immense challenges, setbacks, and victories, but it has undeniably moved American society closer to its founding ideals of equality and liberty for all. Understanding the legacy of the Civil War on civil rights movements is essential for comprehending the ongoing fight for civil rights in the present day and working towards a more just and equitable future.

Role of the government in ensuring equality

One of the primary ways in which the government ensures equality is through legislative measures. It is the responsibility of the government to create and enforce laws that prohibit discrimination and guarantee equal treatment for all individuals. By enacting legislation that prohibits discrimination on the basis of race, gender, religion, disability, or any other grounds, governments set the framework for a more just society. These laws create a level playing field and provide legal recourse to individuals who have been subjected to discrimination or inequality.

Furthermore, the government plays a vital role in ensuring equal access to education and healthcare. Education is a powerful tool that can empower individuals and enable them to break free from the cycle of poverty. By investing in comprehensive and inclusive education systems, the government ensures that all individuals, irrespective of their socio-economic background, have equal opportunities to succeed. Similarly, the government's involvement in healthcare ensures that access to quality healthcare is not determined by one's financial means. By implementing policies that provide affordable healthcare, the government ensures that everyone has equal access to essential medical services.

In addition to legal and policy measures, the government also supports equality through affirmative action initiatives. Affirmative action refers to policies aimed at promoting opportunities for historically disadvantaged groups. These policies seek to redress historical inequalities and create a more representative and inclusive society. The government can implement affirmative action measures in areas such as employment, education, and public contracting, among others. By actively promoting diversity and inclusion, the government helps to level the playing field for marginalized groups and ensures that they have equal opportunities to succeed.

Moreover, the government plays a crucial role in combating systemic barriers and promoting social justice. Systemic barriers refer to structural obstacles that prevent certain groups from fully participating and achieving equality. These barriers can manifest in various forms, including economic inequalities, unequal access to resources, and institutional biases. To address these barriers, the government must actively identify and dismantle systemic inequalities. This can be done by implementing policies that promote social and economic mobility, reducing income disparities, and promoting fairness in resource allocation. By addressing systemic barriers, the government ensures that individuals from all backgrounds have an equal chance to thrive and contribute to society.

The government's role in ensuring equality also extends to addressing environmental justice. Environmental justice recognizes that certain communities, particularly marginalized and low-income groups, bear a disproportionate burden of environmental hazards and pollution. To address this issue, the government must ensure equitable access to clean air, water, and a healthy environment for all citizens. This requires the development of sustainable and inclusive policies that prioritize the well-being of all communities, regardless of their socio-economic status or geographic location. By integrating environmental justice into policy-making, the government can ensure that no group is left behind and that everyone has an equal right to a safe and healthy environment. Through legislative measures, equitable access to education and healthcare, affirmative action initiatives, addressing systemic barriers, and promoting environmental justice, the government can create a society that upholds the principles of fairness and justice. By actively working towards equality, the government fosters an environment where individuals from all backgrounds can thrive and contribute to the betterment of society. It is imperative for governments to recognize their role and commit to fostering equality as a core value, for only then can we truly achieve a just and inclusive society.

Chapter 19: The Road to Reconciliation

EFFORTS TO HEAL THE nation

In times of great division and turmoil, healing the nation becomes an imperative task, calling for concerted efforts from all members of society. It requires a collective commitment to finding common ground, fostering understanding, and implementing transformative solutions that address the root causes of division. This topic carries immense significance, especially in today's interconnected world, where conflicts and unrest can quickly escalate and have far-reaching consequences. By examining the various approaches and strategies aimed at healing the nation, we can gain valuable insights into the restoration of unity, social cohesion, and progress.

Healing a nation encompasses much more than merely papering over wounds or suppressing dissenting voices. It necessitates a sincere recognition of the underlying grievances and injustices that fuel division and a genuine desire to address them. This process starts with acknowledging the pain and suffering endured by different segments of the population and fostering empathetic connections across societal divides. It calls for a compassionate approach that respects the inherent dignity of all individuals, regardless of their background or beliefs.

One critical avenue for healing the nation is through open and inclusive dialogue. This entails creating spaces where people from all walks of life can engage in respectful conversations, share their perspectives, and actively listen to others. Meaningful dialogue is not about changing one's mind or converting others to a specific viewpoint; rather, it aims to promote understanding, empathy, and finding common ground. Such discussions can take place at local community centers, schools, workplaces, or even online platforms, providing opportunities for individuals to meet, exchange ideas, and develop a shared vision for the future. By fostering dialogue, we can bridge the gaps created by misinformation, fear, and suspicion, enabling us to forge a path towards unity.

Furthermore, efforts to heal the nation require the active participation of both the government and civil society. The government plays a pivotal role in creating an enabling environment for healing through the implementation of policies that promote inclusivity, equity, and justice. By addressing systemic issues such as economic inequality, racial discrimination, or social exclusion, governments can begin to dismantle the barriers that perpetuate divisions within society. Simultaneously, civil society organizations, including non-governmental organizations, community-based groups, and grassroots initiatives, play a crucial role in mobilizing communities and advocating for change. Their efforts often focus on providing support, resources, and platforms for marginalized and disadvantaged groups, empowering them to become active agents in the healing process.

Education also plays a central role in healing the nation. By equipping individuals with critical thinking skills, promoting cultural understanding, and fostering a sense of shared history, education can contribute to a more informed and empathetic citizenry. Introducing comprehensive curricula that reflect a diverse range of voices and experiences can help combat ignorance and prejudice, opening minds to different perspectives. Moreover, integrating conflict resolution and mediation training within educational systems can empower future generations with the tools necessary to navigate differences peacefully and meaningfully contribute to national healing efforts.

Media, both traditional and digital, significantly shape public discourse and can either contribute to division or foster unity. Responsible journalism that prioritizes accuracy, objectivity, and fairness is vital for the healing process. Media outlets should strive to provide diverse and well-rounded coverage, amplifying marginalized voices and shedding light on systemic issues that perpetuate division. Moreover, promoting media literacy initiatives that teach individuals to critically evaluate information sources can help counter the spread of misinformation, reducing polarization and building a foundation of trust within society.

While healing the nation requires comprehensive efforts from all stakeholders, it is crucial to ensure that marginalized communities are not left behind. Historically disadvantaged groups, such as racial or ethnic minorities, refugees, or indigenous populations, often bear the brunt of social divisions. Therefore, targeted efforts should be directed towards addressing their unique challenges, healing historical wounds, and empowering them to participate fully in the nation's healing process. By prioritizing the needs of these communities, we foster a more inclusive and equitable society for all. By fostering inclusive dialogue, implementing effective policies, prioritizing education, fostering responsible media practices, and empowering marginalized communities, we create a path towards unity, social cohesion, and progress. Healing is not a singular event but rather a continuous process that requires ongoing dedication. By collectively embracing this task, we can pave the way for a brighter future, where bridges are built, wounds are mended, and nations thrive with shared purpose and understanding.

Rebuilding the South

One of the key challenges in rebuilding the South was the extensive damage to infrastructure. Roads, railways, and buildings had been destroyed, and the agricultural landscape lay in ruins. To address this, a concerted effort was made to repair and rebuild the damaged infrastructure. The federal government, under the leadership of President Abraham Lincoln and later President Andrew Johnson, established programs and initiatives to fund reconstruction projects, focusing on rehabilitating transportation networks and public facilities. Additionally, private investors and philanthropists played a significant role in investing in the region's new infrastructure.

Alongside physical reconstruction, social and economic rebuilding was equally crucial. The system of slavery had been abolished, but the region still grappled with deep-seated racial tensions and inequalities. Reconstruction offered an opportunity for the South to redefine its social fabric and establish a more equitable society. The passage of the Thirteenth, Fourteenth, and Fifteenth Amendments to the United States Constitution represented a transformative step in guaranteeing freedom and civil rights to African Americans. These amendments abolished slavery, granted citizenship rights, and extended suffrage to African American men.

However, despite these transformative amendments, Reconstruction faced significant challenges as it grappled with opposing political factions, resistance from former Confederate leaders, and a lack of resources. This resulted in a complex and uneven process of social and economic change in the South. The Republican Party, which championed the cause of Reconstruction, faced opposition from white Democrats who sought to maintain their pre-war power structures. This led to a period known as the Reconstruction Era, which was marred by violence, political maneuvering, and the rise of white supremacist organizations such as the Ku Klux Klan. These reactionary forces aimed to undo the advances made by Reconstruction and reinstate white supremacy.

Economically, the South relied heavily on agriculture, primarily cotton production, which had been severely disrupted by the war. The labor-intensive plantation system, which had relied on enslaved African Americans, was no longer feasible. The challenge of rebuilding the South's economy lay in transitioning from a system based on coerced labor to one that embraced free labor and diversification. Efforts were made to provide assistance to former slaves in gaining education, acquiring land, and accessing job opportunities. Additionally, northern investors played a crucial role in jump-starting the Southern economy by investing in businesses and industries. This infusion of capital helped initiate a shift toward industrialization in the South.

Despite these efforts, Reconstruction gradually faltered as political will waned, and the South descended into a period of racial segregation and discrimination known as the Jim Crow era. This marked a regression from the advances made during Reconstruction, as African Americans faced legal barriers and pervasive discrimination. The Southern economy continued to struggle, with the region lagging behind the rest of the country in terms of industrial development and economic prosperity.

In recent years, historians and scholars have revisited the legacy of Reconstruction, recognizing both its achievements and failures. While the period was marked by significant obstacles and setbacks, it also laid the groundwork for subsequent civil rights movements and the ongoing struggle for racial equality. The efforts made during Reconstruction to establish legal protections and extend rights to African Americans provided a blueprint for future activists and leaders in their fight for social justice.

Today, the South stands as a region that has undergone tremendous change and growth since the tumultuous years of Reconstruction. The scars of the Civil War and the challenges faced during the rebuilding process continue to shape the region's identity. Through education, dialogue, and a commitment to social progress, the South has the opportunity to further heal the wounds of the past and work towards a more inclusive and equitable future. It was a period of immense challenges, as the region sought to rebuild physically, socially, and economically. While progress was made towards creating a more equitable society, the forces of resistance and prejudice ultimately undermined many of these gains. Nonetheless, Reconstruction left an indelible imprint on American history and provided a foundation for the ongoing struggle for equality. By studying and understanding this pivotal era, we can learn valuable lessons about the complexities of rebuilding after a devastating conflict and the enduring importance of upholding democratic values.

Reunification of the country

When we speak of reunification, we must first consider the historical context in which it occurs. There have been numerous examples throughout history, such as the reunification of Germany in 1990, the reunification of Vietnam in 1976, and the reunification of Yemen in 1990. Each of these instances represents a unique set of circumstances, driven by social, political, and economic factors. Understanding the historical backdrop is crucial in comprehending the complexities and challenges involved in the reunification process.

One of the most significant challenges faced during the reunification process is the reconciliation of differences between the previously divided regions. These differences can be rooted in political ideologies, socioeconomic disparities, cultural divides, or even historical grievances. Reunification often involves bringing these different factions together, facilitating dialogue, and building new structures that accommodate the needs and aspirations of all parties involved. It requires a delicate balance of compromise, negotiation, and strategic decision-making to foster unity and avert further conflict.

Another pressing challenge is the resolution of past conflicts and addressing the legacy of division. Reunification can stir up unresolved issues, rekindling tensions and grievances that lie dormant during periods of separation. It is essential for a reunifying country to establish truth and reconciliation commissions, offering a platform for victims of past conflicts to tell their stories, seek justice, and heal from past traumas. This process allows a society to collectively confront its past, learn from it, and forge a shared understanding of history.

Social integration and the establishment of shared values and national identity are also critical aspects of the reunification process. When regions or territories are separated, they may develop distinct identities and ways of life. Reunification necessitates the creation of a common vision that transcends previous boundaries, fostering a sense of belonging and unity among all citizens. This can be achieved through educational reforms, cultural exchange programs, and the promotion of inclusive national symbols or events that celebrate the diversity within the country.

Economic integration is equally significant in the reunification process. Often, during periods of division, economic disparities arise between the separated regions or territories. Reunification presents an opportunity to address these disparities and foster economic development across the entire country. This can be achieved through investment in infrastructure, the establishment of fair economic policies, and the creation of equal opportunities for all citizens. Economic stability and a shared prosperity contribute to the overall success of the reunified country and lessen the chances of renewed conflicts.

The impacts of reunification can be far-reaching and transformative. A successful reunification process can lead to social cohesion, economic growth, and enhanced regional stability. It has the potential to strengthen a nation both domestically and internationally, forging a unified voice and identity on the global stage. Reunification can also inspire neighboring countries or regions facing similar divisions, offering a model for peaceful resolution and cooperation. It involves reconciling differences, addressing past conflicts, fostering a shared identity, and promoting economic integration. However, the rewards of successful reunification are immense, with the potential to transform a divided nation into a united and prosperous one. The lessons and experiences gained from previous reunifications serve as invaluable resources for countries or regions embarking on a similar path.

Chapter 20: Conclusion

REFLECTION ON THE IMPACT of the Civil War

Lasting from 1861 to 1865, it marked a turning point in the nation's development and had a profound impact on the lives of individuals, communities, and indeed the entire nation. This piece aims to reflect on the various aspects and consequences of the Civil War, exploring its social, economic, and political impact on the United States.

1. Social Impact:

The social impact of the Civil War cannot be understated. The conflict tore families and communities apart, pitting brothers against brothers and friends against friends. It highlighted and intensified existing divisions between the North and the South, deeply impacting societal norms and relationships. Slavery, a central issue at the heart of the war, symbolized the stark dichotomy between free and slave states. The subsequent Emancipation Proclamation and the passage of the Thirteenth Amendment forever altered the social fabric of the nation by abolishing slavery. However, the deep-rooted racial tensions and disparities that resulted from this dark one in our history continue to be felt to this day.

2. Economic Impact:

The economic impact of the Civil War was far-reaching. The conflict, fueled by sectional economic differences, devastated Southern agriculture and industry. The South relied heavily on slave labor, and when slavery was abolished, the economic machinery of the region suffered greatly. Additionally, the destruction caused by the battles, particularly in the South, led to widespread infrastructure damage and loss of productive capacity. Conversely, the North experienced unprecedented industrial growth as it supplied troops with arms, ammunition, and other supplies. This shift laid the foundation for the Industrial Revolution and marked the rise of the United States as an industrial powerhouse.

3. Political Impact:

The Civil War had a profound impact on the political landscape of the United States. At its core, the war was a struggle to preserve and define the nation's identity and purpose, ultimately leading to a reaffirmation of the principles outlined in the Declaration of Independence. The Confederacy's attempt to secede from the Union tested the strength and durability of the United States as a democratic republic. The subsequent victory of the Union led to the consolidation of federal power, with the federal government becoming the ultimate authority over individual states. Moreover, the Reconstruction Era following the war attempted to redress the deep-seated racial injustices through several constitutional amendments aimed at securing civil rights for African Americans.

4. Cultural Impact:

The Civil War left an indelible mark on American culture. The war's horrific casualties and sheer scale shattered romantic notions of warfare and forever transformed the perception of armed conflict. This period saw the emergence of a new brand of literature known as "Civil War literature," which sought to capture the war's devastating realities and often grappled with themes of loss, sacrifice, and the moral complexities of war. Additionally, the war further entrenched the concept of American exceptionalism, as the nation reconciled the ideals of freedom and equality with the harsh realities brought to light by the war.

IN REFLECTION, THE impact of the American Civil War was multifaceted and echoed through virtually every aspect of American life. It reshaped the nation socially, economically, politically, and culturally, leaving an enduring legacy that continues to influence us today. Understanding and reflecting upon this pivotal moment in history is crucial for comprehending the struggles and progress our nation has undergone and the ongoing quest for a more just and unified society. By examining the consequences of the Civil War, we can learn from the mistakes of the past and strive to build a future rooted in equality, peace, and understanding.

Lessons learned from this period in American history

CIVIL WAR POLITICS: THE DIVIDED NATION AND ITS LEADERS

The period in American history that we are discussing refers to the years between 1865 and 1898, encompassing the aftermath of the Civil War and the subsequent era of Reconstruction. This was a tumultuous time for the nation, as it grappled with the challenges of rebuilding the nation, healing the wounds of war, and confronting new social, economic, and political realities. From this period of history, several important lessons can be learned that continue to shape and inform our understanding of America today.

One significant lesson we can draw from this period is the importance of unity and reconciliation in times of division and strife. Following the Civil War, the wounds inflicted on the nation were deep and profound. This period tested the resilience of the American people and highlighted the necessity of finding common ground and embracing a shared vision of the future. The process of Reconstruction, though imperfect, attempted to foster this unity by advocating for the rights and freedoms of all citizens, irrespective of their race. The lesson here is that no matter how great the divide, it is essential to come together and work towards a common goal for the betterment of society as a whole.

Another crucial lesson we can take from this period is the need for continued progress and social change. During the late 19th century, significant strides were made towards equality and justice. The passage of the 13th, 14th, and 15th Amendments extended civil rights and protections to formerly enslaved African Americans. However, it is important to note that these gains were not without significant setbacks and challenges. The rise of Jim Crow laws and the institutionalization of racial segregation in the South illustrate the constant struggle for equal rights. This period reminds us that progress is not guaranteed, and we must remain vigilant in our pursuit of justice and equality for all.

Additionally, the era following the Civil War taught us valuable lessons about the power and limitations of the federal government. While the federal government played a critical role in initiating Reconstruction and enacting civil rights legislation, its ability to enforce and secure these changes was limited. As the federal government began to withdraw its support for Reconstruction in the 1870s, many gains made towards racial equality were eroded. This highlights the need for a strong and committed federal government that is willing to take decisive action to protect the rights of all citizens. It also emphasizes the importance of holding those in power accountable for ensuring justice and equality.

One lesson that emerged from this period is the recognition that economic prosperity cannot come at the expense of marginalized communities. The rapid industrialization and expansion of the United States during this time led to substantial economic growth. However, this growth was often achieved through the exploitation of vulnerable populations, such as immigrant workers and sharecroppers. The stark disparities between the wealthy industrialists and the impoverished working class led to increased social unrest and the rise of labor movements. This period teaches us that economic progress must be accompanied by fair labor practices, regulations to protect workers' rights, and measures to alleviate income inequality.

Furthermore, this period in American history underscored the importance of education as a tool for social progress and equal opportunity. African Americans and newly freed slaves recognized the power of education in securing their future and breaking the cycle of poverty and oppression. Institutions such as historically black colleges and universities were founded during this time to provide educational opportunities for African Americans who had been previously denied access to formal education. The lesson here is the transformative power of education in empowering individuals and communities to overcome adversity and achieve social mobility. The importance of unity and reconciliation, the need for continued progress and social change, the power and limitations of the federal government, the imperative of economic fairness and labor rights, and the transformative power of education are all vital lessons that emerged from this transformative era. By reflecting on and learning from these lessons, we can work towards a more equitable, just, and inclusive society for all.